Advertising: A Very Short Introduction

VERY SHORT INTRODUCTIONS are for anyone wanting a stimulating and accessible way in to a new subject. They are written by experts, and have been published in more than 25 languages worldwide.

The series began in 1995, and now represents a wide variety of topics in history, philosophy, religion, science, and the humanities. The VSI Library now contains over 200 volumes—a Very Short Introduction to everything from ancient Egypt and Indian philosophy to conceptual art and cosmology—and will continue to grow to a library of around 300 titles.

Very Short Introductions available now:

ADVERTISING Winston Fletcher
AFRICAN HISTORY
   John Parker and Richard Rathbone
AMERICAN POLITICAL PARTIES
   AND ELECTIONS L. Sandy Maisel
THE AMERICAN
   PRESIDENCY Charles O. Jones
ANARCHISM Colin Ward
ANCIENT EGYPT Ian Shaw
ANCIENT PHILOSOPHY Julia Annas
ANCIENT WARFARE
   Harry Sidebottom
ANGLICANISM Mark Chapman
THE ANGLO-SAXON AGE John Blair
ANIMAL RIGHTS David DeGrazia
ANTISEMITISM Steven Beller
THE APOCRYPHAL GOSPELS
   Paul Foster
ARCHAEOLOGY Paul Bahn
ARCHITECTURE Andrew Ballantyne
ARISTOTLE Jonathan Barnes
ART HISTORY Dana Arnold
ART THEORY Cynthia Freeland
ATHEISM Julian Baggini
AUGUSTINE Henry Chadwick
AUTISM Uta Frith
BARTHES Jonathan Culler
BESTSELLERS John Sutherland
THE BIBLE John Riches
BIBLICAL ARCHEOLOGY Eric H. Cline
BIOGRAPHY Hermione Lee
THE BOOK OF MORMON
   Terryl Givens
THE BRAIN Michael O'Shea

BRITISH POLITICS Anthony Wright
BUDDHA Michael Carrithers
BUDDHISM Damien Keown
BUDDHIST ETHICS Damien Keown
CAPITALISM James Fulcher
CATHOLICISM Gerald O'Collins
THE CELTS Barry Cunliffe
CHAOS Leonard Smith
CHOICE THEORY Michael Allingham
CHRISTIAN ART Beth Williamson
CHRISTIANITY Linda Woodhead
CITIZENSHIP Richard Bellamy
CLASSICAL MYTHOLOGY
   Helen Morales
CLASSICS Mary Beard and John Henderson
CLAUSEWITZ Michael Howard
THE COLD WAR Robert McMahon
COMMUNISM Leslie Holmes
CONSCIOUSNESS Susan Blackmore
CONTEMPORARY ART
   Julian Stallabrass
CONTINENTAL PHILOSOPHY
   Simon Critchley
COSMOLOGY Peter Coles
THE CRUSADES Christopher Tyerman
CRYPTOGRAPHY
   Fred Piper and Sean Murphy
DADA AND SURREALISM
   David Hopkins
DARWIN Jonathan Howard
THE DEAD SEA SCROLLS Timothy Lim
DEMOCRACY Bernard Crick
DESCARTES Tom Sorell
DESERTS Nick Middleton

STATISTICS David J. Hand
STUART BRITAIN John Morrill
SUPERCONDUCTIVITY
 Stephen Blundell
TERRORISM Charles Townshend
THEOLOGY David F. Ford
THOMAS AQUINAS Fergus Kerr
TRAGEDY Adrian Poole
THE TUDORS John Guy
TWENTIETH-CENTURY BRITAIN
 Kenneth O. Morgan

THE UNITED NATIONS
 Jussi M. Hanhimäki
THE VIKINGS Julian Richards
WITCHCRAFT Malcolm Gaskill
WITTGENSTEIN A. C. Grayling
WORLD MUSIC Philip Bohlman
THE WORLD TRADE
 ORGANIZATION
 Amrita Narlikar
WRITING AND SCRIPT
 Andrew Robinson

Available soon:

FILM MUSIC
 Kathryn Kalinak
FORENSIC PSYCHOLOGY
 David Canter
MODERNISM
 Christopher Butler

LEADERSHIP
 Keith Grint
CHRISTIAN ETHICS
 D. Stephen Long

For more information visit our website
www.oup.co.uk/general/vsi/

Winston Fletcher

ADVERTISING

A Very Short Introduction

OXFORD

UNIVERSITY PRESS

Great Clarendon Street, Oxford OX2 6DP

Oxford University Press is a department of the University of Oxford.
It furthers the University's objective of excellence in research, scholarship,
and education by publishing worldwide in

Oxford New York

Auckland Cape Town Dar es Salaam Hong Kong Karachi
Kuala Lumpur Madrid Melbourne Mexico City Nairobi
New Delhi Shanghai Taipei Toronto

With offices in

Argentina Austria Brazil Chile Czech Republic France Greece
Guatemala Hungary Italy Japan Poland Portugal Singapore
South Korea Switzerland Thailand Turkey Ukraine Vietnam

Oxford is a registered trade mark of Oxford University Press
in the UK and in certain other countries

Published in the United States
by Oxford University Press Inc., New York

© Winston Fletcher 2010

The moral rights of the author have been asserted
Database right Oxford University Press (maker)

First published 2010

British Library Cataloguing in Publication Data

Data available

Library of Congress Cataloging in Publication Data

Data available

Typeset by SPI Publisher Services, Pondicherry, India
Printed in Great Britain
on acid-free paper by
Ashford Colour Press Ltd, Gosport, Hampshire

ISBN 978-0-19-956892-5

1 3 5 7 9 10 8 6 4 2

Contents

Preface

Advertising is riddled with myths and misunderstandings.
It is simultaneously believed to be both immensely powerful
and immensely wasteful, to increase economic prosperity and
to be morally questionable. Neither its historic origins nor its
modern operations are well understood. Many of these myths
and misunderstandings are almost as widespread within the
advertising industry – itself something of a myth, as we shall
see – as they are among the public at large. This short book,
written by someone with extensive knowledge of advertising
from the inside, corrects and clarifies the misunderstandings
that are so common.

List of illustrations

Chapter 1
What does advertising do?

What is advertising?

Like many other commonplace words – think of art, love, and justice, for example – advertising is surprisingly hard to define with precision. First, there is the difference between advertising and advertisements: advertising is a process, advertisements are the end result of that process, but the words are often used interchangeably. Second, and perhaps more importantly, while the public uses the word 'advertising' to cover all kinds of publicity, within the advertising industry the word is used fairly specifically (though even here, confusions arise).

In this *Very Short Introduction*, I shall be using the industry definition. Within the industry, advertising is just one type of marketing communication. Other types of marketing communication that are *not* normally defined as advertising include: packaging; sales promotions (money-offs, two-for-ones, competitions, and the like); catalogues; shop windows and in-store publicity; brand placements in television programmes and films; commercial emails; brand names on clothes and other goods; public relations (brand mentions in the media); commercial websites and blogs; and telephone selling. All of these (and many others), are marketing communications, and are often used to increase the sales of things. But within the industry they are not defined as advertisements, nor as advertising.

So what exactly is an advertisement? Though it is a mite blurred at the edges, a good working definition is:

> An advertisement is a paid-for communication intended to inform and/or persuade one or more people.

Let's examine the key words in this definition.

First: *'paid-for'*. An advertisement that is not paid-for is not, strictly, an advertisement at all. If no cost whatsoever is involved then the communication may be good publicity, and it may be persuasive, but it is not technically advertising – unless it is an advertisement that has deliberately been given away free (perhaps to a charity, or something similar).

Second: *'communication'*. Every advertisement attempts to bridge a gap between the sender and the receiver. This bridge is a communication. To buy a whole page in a newspaper and leave it blank is not to advertise. Whether in words or pictures, or usually both, advertisements must communicate something to whoever sees or hears them.

Third: *'intended'*. As we shall see, particularly in Chapter 7, not all advertisements 'work' in the sense of achieving their intended aims. The fact that an advertisement does not achieve its aims does not detract from it being an advertisement. It is the intention that counts.

Fourth: *'inform and/or persuade'*. Many people, usually critics hostile to advertising, have tried to draw a distinction between *informative* advertising and *persuasive* advertising. The former is deemed to be acceptable and desirable, the latter to be less acceptable or even totally unacceptable. In reality the line between information and persuasion is impossible to draw. All the information an advertiser includes in an advertisement is intended to be persuasive (unless it is there because it is legally necessary).

But as the persuasive role of advertising is contentious, it is better to say that all advertisements aim to '*inform and/or persuade*'. However, an advertisement that aimed to have no persuasive influence whatsoever would, again, hardly be an advertisement.

Finally: '*one or more people*'. All advertisements are addressed to people. Sometimes to just one person ('*Lollipop – be my Valentine and I will be yours forever. Muscleman*'); sometimes to countless millions ('*L'Oreal. Because You're Worth It*'). When the public thinks about advertising, it almost always thinks about mass advertising, in mass media – the type of advertising on which we will concentrate in this book. But small, classified advertisements are a huge advertising sector, particularly in printed media and on the Internet, and must never be forgotten. In Britain and many other countries, over 40% of the advertising revenue of printed media comes from classifieds, though this percentage is falling sharply throughout the world, as the Internet is winning lots of classified advertising away from more traditional media.

It has been important to sort out this definition because many things that are popularly considered to be advertisements will hardly be touched upon in this book. The focus will be on mass consumer advertising in the major media – television, newspapers and magazines, posters, radio, cinema, and the Internet: in other words, what most people mean by advertising, most of the time.

What does advertising do?

Another apparently simple and boring question: surely everyone knows advertising sells things – that is its purpose, isn't it? But is it really so simple? How about *Muscleman*? What was he trying to sell to *Lollipop*? When charities advertise for funds, what are they selling? When the government advertises to stop people smoking, or drinking and driving, or to give blood, what are they selling? When the army, or the NHS, or any business, advertises to recruit people, what are they selling? In every case, the advertisements

1. What are they selling?

are intended to '*inform and/or persuade*', so they fall squarely within our definition. But are they really *selling* things?

This leads to a fundamental feature of advertising which many people find difficult to grasp. Advertising is not a homogeneous entity. (That is why it is so hard to define with precision.) It covers a multitude of diverse types of communication, with equally diverse objectives. Most advertisements, it is true, aim to sell goods and services. But not all do. And even those that do, aim to achieve sales in a host of varying ways. Advertisements are like the bits and pieces in a kaleidoscope. Together they appear to make a unified pattern – but in reality each one of them is likely to be quite different from the others.

Everyone who works in advertising gets used to outsiders asking: 'What makes an advertising campaign successful? What is the secret of effective advertising?' – or something very similar. The question implies there must be some kind of 'Golden Key', which advertisers can use to unlock the secret of producing advertising that works. But there is no Golden Key – and there is no single answer to the question 'What makes an advertising campaign successful?' (Though the people who ask it are nearly always keen to proffer an answer of their own, which is why they ask the question in the first place.)

There could never be a Golden Key, because even campaigns that are specifically intended to sell things do so in a multitude of different ways, with a multitude of different immediate objectives. Here are ten common ones, used by different advertisers at different times for different products and brands (we will look closely at the difference between a 'product' and a 'brand' in Chapter 3). The list is not comprehensive, and could never be, as advertisers are constantly inventing new objectives. However, a campaign may be intended to:

- launch a completely new brand;
- launch a new product into an existing brand – a 'line extension';
- promote an improvement to an existing brand;

- make people who have not heard of a brand become aware of it;
- persuade people who know of a brand but haven't tried it to try it;
- persuade ex-users of a brand to try it again;
- persuade current users to use it more often;
- persuade current users to try using it in different ways;
- persuade a different target market – younger or wealthier perhaps – to use the brand;
- persuade retailers to stock the brand, so people can easily buy it.

These varying objectives demand varied messages, and so demand an almost infinite variety of advertising approaches.

Many textbooks argue that it is vital to define the single objective of any campaign with precision, and in detail, before running a campaign. Advertising that tries to be all things to all people, they argue, always fails.

Well it is certainly essential to define the objectives of any campaign with precision, and in detail – but a campaign may well have more than one single objective, as long as the different objectives are consistent with each other and are in no way mutually contradictory. Indeed, recent research has shown that most successful campaigns have, on average, approximately two-and-a-half overlapping objectives, for example 'To build awareness among affluent prospective customers of an exclusive new brand which they will find only in top-quality retailers'. (That particular objective includes no fewer than four overlapping objectives – to build awareness/among affluent customers/of an exclusive brand/only available in top-quality retailers – and all of them are essential to achieve the brand's entire goal.)

The advertising strategy

The objectives of any campaign will be spelled out in a crucial document generally called the *advertising strategy*. This is a key blueprint in the creation of new campaigns, and we will return to it frequently throughout the book. Different advertisers and their agencies give it different names, but its purposes are always the same: to define the objectives of the advertising campaign, and to ensure everyone involved in producing the campaign knows exactly what these are. This will ensure that they all (many of them highly paid creative people) waste no time developing ideas that are irrelevant or are not what is required.

To achieve these purposes, the advertising strategy will have a raft of subheadings and boxes which must be completed before any work on the campaign goes ahead. These subheadings/boxes will precisely define the blueprint of the campaign. They will include the campaign's objectives; facts about the brand that show the objectives to be realistic; the brand's competitors, with details of their advertising and marketing campaigns; a summary of any relevant market research – saying why consumers use the brand, and why they do not; the message the campaign must communicate, and the tone in which it must be communicated; which media are likely to be used for the campaign; the budgets available both for the preparation of the advertisements and for the media campaign; a timescale for both the preparation of the advertisements and for the duration of the media campaign when it runs; any other details felt to be important to the campaign in question; and, particularly, the *target market* at which the campaign will aim.

Many of these important headings will be expanded upon in the chapters that follow. But because of its crucial importance, let us start with the last first: the *target market*.

What is a target market?

The two most important facts about an advertising campaign are the brand itself – that is, the product or service being advertised – and its potential purchasers, its target market. You might think the former to be far more important than the latter, and this would undoubtedly have been the view in years gone by. But today the two are seen to be symbiotic: the brand and its target market are inextricably entwined.

How come? There are three factors involved. First, the ever-burgeoning diversity of products and services in every field means that even the largest, most popular brands are used only by minority segments of the population. Even a massive supermarket chain like Tesco is used regularly by only about one-third of the British population. So advertisers need to find out everything they possibly can about the exact segment of the population they are targeting. Second, the growth of market research allows advertisers to know who their potential customers are with much greater precision than used to be the case. And third, media audiences are themselves now so segmented it is essential to specify the target market in order to advertise in the media which will reach them most

2. **Even a massive retail chain like Tesco is used regularly by only about one-third of the British population**

cost-effectively. The days when one advertisement in a single newspaper like the *News of the World* (in 1948, the *News of the World* reached a world-record sale of 8,000,000 copies weekly), or on a single channel like ITV, could reach more than 50% of the British population are long gone. (Today, even with mass media like television, different types of people watch different channels, different programmes, and at different times of day: there is no point in advertising to busy business people, on a channel they do not watch, in the middle of the afternoon, for example.)

The outcome of these three factors has been that products and services are no longer designed and formulated for 100% of the population. They are designed for specific target markets: clearly defined population sectors, large and small. This is the basis of the symbiosis between the brand and its target market.

3. In 1948, the *News of the World* reached a world record sale of 8,000,000 copies weekly

To analyse and understand their target markets, all major advertisers nowadays carry out considerable market research, honed to their own particular needs. But there are also sizable syndicated surveys available, which are continuous, and which anyone can obtain under contract. Of these, probably the most important is the *Target Group Index* (TGI). TGI was launched in Britain in 1969, but it is now a global research operation run in over 50 countries by Kantar Market Research, a subsidiary of WPP, one of the world's largest marketing services conglomerates.

TGI today carries out over 700,000 annual interviews in the countries where it operates, and it identifies the detailed demographic profiles of the users of over 4,000 brands in more than 500 product fields. It will identify their age, class, sex, marital status, working status, education, regional habitation, media consumption, and social activities. But TGI goes much further. It analyses each brand's frequency of use: do its consumers use the brand often ('heavy users') or infrequently ('light users')? It analyses consumers' opinions and attitudes to 250 questions covering health, holidays, finance, the environment, and many other subjects, correlating this invaluable psychographic and personality data with brand usage. TGI collects and provides all this data because it knows it to be the information advertisers, media, and agencies (its own target markets) will require in order to learn as much as possible about *their* target markets.

The TGI data helps advertisers and their agencies identify those consumers who are potentially the most likely sources of sales: the target market. But it will also reveal the target market's attitudes to the brand. What do consumers want from the brand, and what do they not want? This again reflects the symbiotic relationship between the brand and its target market. The brand only exists to provide its target market with what it wants. So let us now explore what consumers want from their brands.

What do customers want from their brands? Facts or images?

Yet another seemingly simple and silly question, you may feel! Surely people just want the things they buy to do what they say they are going to do, efficiently and reliably: to be 'fit for purpose', as consumer protection laws state.

Not quite. Another effect of the symbiosis between brands and their target markets has been a shift of emphasis away from product formulations, and towards *end-benefits*. Put simply, people do not buy drills because they want drills, they buy drills because they want holes. Unless you are a metallurgist, when you buy a drill its metallic specification will be unimportant to you. You don't care about its metallic specification – you just need some holes. It is astonishing how often policymakers fail to grasp this vital fact. Take a look at a petfood pack, for example. Petfood manufacturers are legally required to publish exact ingredient specifications on their packs – though pet owners care only about the end-benefits: that their pets will enjoy the petfood and will stay healthy. The detailed specifications mean nothing to them.

And because human beings (and pets) vary, the end-benefits which different groups of people require from similar products inevitably vary too. So the different groups comprise different target markets. And advertising campaigns will need to promote the differing end-benefits that each of the target markets requires.

Naturally advertisers have always appreciated that different people want different things, and that people buy goods for the benefits they provide. But if you look at any book of 19th-century advertisements – try Leonard de Vries's excellent *Victorian Advertisements*, for example – you will quickly see that in those days almost all advertisements concentrated on the product itself and how it functioned. Today most advertising campaigns concentrate on end-benefits. Product ingredients and formulations will only be mentioned to back up and justify the end-benefits the product provides.

And – especially in an affluent society – the benefits that consumers want from products are not only factual and functional. Consumers want and expect psychological and emotional, as well as functional, end-benefits from the goods they buy. Yes, they want them to function properly, to be 'fit for purpose', that goes without saying. But they also want their purchases to make them feel good, in any number of ways. In advertising terms, they want the *brand image* to be right for them. The *brand image* is the halo of feelings and emotions that brands inspire. Consumers may want the image of a brand they buy to make them feel more glamorous, or younger, or cleverer, or in-the-know. They may want their brand's image to make them feel more masculine, or feminine, or more healthy, or a more sensible shopper, or a better parent, or more ecologically conscientious. And these brand image benefits will be crucial to their buying choices.

So the advertising campaign must take account of such emotive benefits – and, once again, these will vary for different target markets. The advertising strategy will define what the target market's emotive requirements are. And nowadays, in many product fields, it is customers' psychological and emotive needs, as much as their functional needs, which a brand and its advertising must cater for. There is clear research evidence that 'emotional' advertisements are, on average, more effective than unembellished factual advertisements. This is particularly true in those markets – unlike drills – where brand imagery is crucial to consumers, markets as diverse as automobiles, airlines, and alcohol; clothes, cosmetics, and carbonated drinks.

None of this is as new as critics of modern advertising contend. It is clear that since earliest history, human beings have been well aware of the imagery – 'the emotional baggage' – of the products and clothes they own and display. But equally, none of this is a charter to produce emotional advertisements that disregard the product itself. It is absolutely vital for a brand's image to be consistent with its functional benefits, and vice versa. Cynics contend that a clever advertising campaign can make the public think whatever the advertiser wants them to think about a brand. Not so. No matter how clever it is, advertising cannot make consumers think a weak beer is strong, or a sweet wine is dry – or a blunt drill will make good holes. Clever (but foolish) advertising may persuade consumers to buy the product once, but they will then quickly discover they have been cheated. The functional and the image benefits that a brand offers, which the advertising must aim to communicate, must interlock as tightly as pieces in a wooden jigsaw. If the pieces do not fit together perfectly, consumers will find the brand confusing, therefore unacceptable, and ultimately self-defeating. It would be akin to an ineffectual leader puffing himself up like a great emperor and then failing to win a battle.

Finally in this section, it is essential to keep in mind the diversity of advertisers and advertising, already emphasized. Most of the above, for simplicity's sake, has related to the advertising of products: goods rather than services. But in most affluent countries, services today account for a major percentage of the gross national product. Indeed, the value of the service sector is now often larger than that of the product sector. In Britain, for example, the service sector accounts for some two-thirds of the economy: retailers, entertainment, financial services, travel, and tourism are huge sectors, and huge advertisers (see table on page 33). Everything written about goods in the paragraphs above applies equally to services. It is just as important to define the service's target market (and TGI covers all major services, as well as products); to define the end-benefits the service offers; to blend factual benefits with emotional benefits; and to communicate the desired brand image. The symbiosis between brand and target market is fundamental in all modern advertising, whatever is being advertised.

How are all these decisions taken?

The brief and truthful answer is: with great difficulty.

John Hobson, one of the most thoughtful and analytical British advertising men of the 20th century, who founded one of the era's most successful advertising agencies in 1955, said:

> In advertising there are always dozens of ways of doing any job.
> We consider them all and then test and test and test until we get
> the right one.

But in the decades since 1955, myriads of campaigns have been tried – and some did the business, while others were found lacking. At the same time, advertisers have carried out literally countless market research studies. This all means that the 'dozens of ways of doing any job' can usually be whittled down in advance, if all the relevant information is carefully studied and analysed. Today the prime responsibility for studying and analysing this information falls to people who are called *account planners*.

Though account planning is now practised globally, it did not come into existence until around 1970, when two London advertising agencies developed it almost simultaneously. The two agencies were J Walter Thomson London, the UK subsidiary of the giant JWT American agency, now owned by the WPP conglomerate; and a then infant British agency called Boase Massimi Pollitt, founded in May 1968. The name 'account planning' came from J Walter Thomson London, and the two agencies developed the system in slightly different ways. Other agencies have since made their own small adjustments, but the fundamentals of the system are universal.

The account planning system demands that an account planner – an analytical researcher – is assigned by the advertising agency to every client. The account planner is not a backroom boffin, as researchers in advertising agencies used to be, but personally represents the agency to its clients at meetings, up front. The account planner will analyse all the available data about the brand to be advertised: sales trends, past research, past campaign results, competitors' activity, consumers' attitudes – everything mentioned above in connection with the advertising strategy blueprint. Having analysed all the data, account planners are then responsible for developing and drafting the detailed advertising strategy: what are the aims and targets of the advertising, how will it achieve them? All of this will need to be agreed by the planner's colleagues in the agency, and then by the client.

With the abundance of data now available, transmuting it all into an effective advertising strategy is not easy. The account planner needs to be highly computer literate and needs skill, experience, and insight to study masses of research and sales information, boil it all down to a few key conclusions, and deduce from these exactly what the advertising campaign must communicate, and to which target market. Simplistic, clichéd conclusions and objectives are useless. If the account planner can say nothing more than that the brand is better than its competitors, and the campaign must persuade the public of this fact, the resulting advertising campaign is likely to be bland to the point of tedium. The planner must be much sharper and go far deeper. What are the brand's real functional and emotional strengths and weaknesses; in which respects is the brand better (or worse) than its competitors? How can all this be persuasively communicated? Which target market, or target markets, must be persuaded? Which arguments – both rational and emotional – should be deployed to persuade them? Talented account planners will put flesh on the bare bones of the data, and make the advertising strategy inspiring and exciting to those who will have to put it into effect. (Unsurprisingly, the best account planners are nowadays highly rewarded – and incidentally, a high percentage of them are female.) Only at this point will the agency's creative teams and the media specialists go to their starting blocks and prepare to get the campaign moving.

The next part of the account planner's task is still more difficult. Once the draft advertising strategy has been agreed, and put into action, it will be the account planner's responsibility to ensure that the resulting campaign meets the strategy's stated objectives. However, we would be jumping too far ahead of ourselves to deal with this process now: we will see how it works in Chapter 7.

First, we must ourselves now do some basic investigation, into the history of advertising, to show how and why it has developed in the ways it has. It is a complex and unusual industry with many separate parts, and to understand how advertising works it is essential to disentangle why it is so split up, and to define what the separate parts do.

Chapter 2
How the advertising industry is structured

Look back in wonder

Like most people, you probably believe advertising is a relatively modern phenomenon – perhaps a century or two old – and that it was invented in America. Both are twaddle.

Advertising shop signs existed some 6,000 years ago, and were common in Rome and throughout the ancient world. But it was the classical Athenians who can probably lay claim to the invention of commercial advertising as we know it today. In Athens, town criers, chosen for their mellifluous voices and clear elocution, strolled through the streets making public proclamations, and interrupted their proclamations with paid-for advertisements (just as advertisements interrupt television newscasts today). Aesclyptoe, an early Athenian cosmetician, used town criers to promote his lotions and potions with consummate professionalism:

> For eyes that are shining, for cheeks like the dawn,
> For beauty that lasts after girlhood has gone,
> For prices in reason the women who know
> Now buy their cosmetics from Aesclyptoe.

This 'jingle' – it was probably sung – could have sprung yesterday from a highly paid London or New York copywriter's laptop.

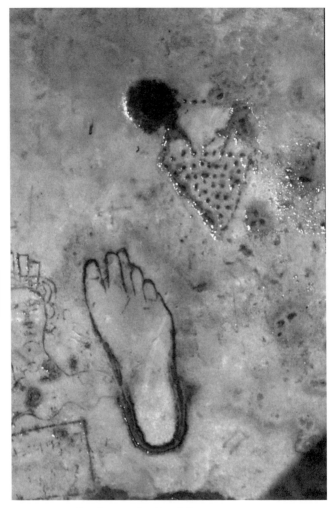

4. A Roman advertisement for a brothel

Following the Athenians, advertising burgeoned in Rome, Herculaneum, and Pompeii, where prostitutes' ads can still be seen carved into the stonework of the once buried city. Thus was one of the world's oldest professions linked with another of the world's oldest professions from the start.

During the 'dark ages' after the fall of the Roman Empire, advertising appears to have disappeared. Then it reappeared, in Britain and France during the 13th century, again being sung by town criers. Printed advertising followed hard upon Gutenberg's invention of the printing press in Germany in about 1450. The first known printed advertisement in English was published in 1477, printed by William Caxton, who had brought printing to Britain a few years earlier. By the start of the 17th century, advertising was already so common that in 1712 the British government introduced a tax of one shilling (a sizable sum) on every advertisement published in a newspaper. But this tax did little to restrain advertising's growth. In 1759, the great lexicographer Dr Samuel Johnson wrote: 'Advertisements are now so numerous they are very negligently perused.' An opinion many people express to this day, without realizing its centuries-old ancestry.

The government's 1712 tax was not repealed until 1853, by which time just under two million newspaper advertisements were being taxed annually. At the same time, a vast number of advertisements were appearing in 'illegal' publications, which were not registered for the tax, plus legal and illegal posters and billboards, and handbills which were pushed into people's fingers as they walked about the streets, along with a galaxy of invented advertising ideas, many of them entertainingly eccentric (one company devised a way to shoot advertisements into people's gardens with a gun). Unsurprisingly, people began complaining, as they have complained ever since, that there was far too much advertising, and that something needed to be done about it. Little was.

5. In 1759, Dr Samuel Johnson wrote 'Advertisements are now so numerous they are very negligently perused.'

Initially advertisements were entirely text, without illustration, and were generally written by the merchant himself. But by the end of the 18th century, specialists in advertisement writing began to appear, as did illustrations. These were produced by people calling themselves 'advertising agents', because they not only wrote and illustrated the advertisements, they also acted as sales agents for the media, selling advertising space to the merchants. Almost certainly the first advertising agent in Britain – and in the world – was William Taylor, who so described himself in an advertisement for his services in 1786. (It is often claimed that the American Volney B. Palmer set up the first advertising agency in 1842 in Philadelphia, but Taylor predated him in London by more than half a century.) And the great essayist Charles Lamb was an early freelance copywriter, raking in a little extra cash by writing advertisements for his friend, the advertising agent James White, during the early 1800s.

The basic three-part structure of the advertising industry in Britain – later to spread throughout the world – was thus established: advertisers, who bought space for their advertisements; media, who sold the space; and agencies, who were middlemen – selling space on behalf of the media, and creating advertisements for the advertisers.

The advertising tripartite

'The advertising industry does not exist', my first boss used to quip. He was not, as you may be thinking, saying that advertising people are not industrious: as in all industries, some are and some are not. He was saying that there is no such entity as the advertising industry. What people call the advertising industry is an amorphous patchwork of different companies and specializations, broadly divisible into its three basic sectors – usually called the 'advertising tripartite'. Though other ways of organizing advertising have been tried over the years, the 'advertising tripartite' structure is now the basis of advertising industries throughout the world, and may be assumed to be the best and most functional way to organize the creation and production of advertising campaigns.

As in the 19th century, the three legs of the advertising tripartite are the advertisers, the media, and the advertising agencies. Let us consider each in turn.

First, the advertisers: retailers, manufacturers, finance companies, charities, governments, loving suitors like *Muscleman*, and countless others. They pay for all the advertising, but advertising is not their principal activity. For them, advertising is a means to an end. It is, as we saw earlier, one of the numerous means of marketing communication. For many, it will be their *main* means of marketing communication, on which they spend considerable sums of money. These will generally be advertisers selling high-volume famous brands to the general public: brands like Coca-Cola, Sony, L'Oreal, Toyota, Tesco, British Airways, and tens of thousands more. Because their target markets are large, they will use mass media to reach them, and advertising in mass media is expensive. But for other advertisers, advertising will be a far smaller component in their marketing communications mix. These will generally be advertisers addressing relatively small, tightly defined target markets. Advertisers in this group will include businesses selling to other businesses rather than to the public; or selling to hobbyists who read specialist hobby magazines and visit specialist websites; or selling to people from a narrow demographic sector like the very old, or the very rich, or owners of unusual pets; or selling to residents in a particular locality, in which the advertiser trades.

Big or small, advertisers are the driving force of the advertising industry. They are the paymasters, they call the tunes, and they want to see results. Yet almost nobody who works for an advertiser thinks of themselves as working 'in advertising'. They work, say, in carbonated drinks (Coca-Cola), or in consumer electronics (Sony), or in toiletries and cosmetics (L'Oreal), or in the automobile industry (Toyota), or in retailing (Tesco), or in travel (British Airways). Within each of those large organizations, there will be people who work full-time, or almost full-time, on their company's advertising. But in a few months or years these people may well be moved to another department within the company. Advertising is, perhaps temporarily, a key part of their professionalism, but it is not their profession. They do not think of themselves as being part of 'the advertising industry'.

The same is largely true of the second leg of the advertising tripartite, the media. The media – in particular, television, print, posters, radio, cinema, and the Internet – carry and publish advertisements in return for advertisers' money. Today the media receive approximately 90% of all the money the advertisers spend. In the past, the media received 85%, and the remaining 15% went to advertising agencies as a fixed-rate commission. Nowadays, that fixed-rate commission system is virtually obsolete. The exact percentages the media receive, and the agencies get paid, are subject to negotiation – but on average, agencies get about 10%, rather than 15%, of the total, and the media receive the rest.

Television, radio, cinema, and posters carry, almost exclusively, display advertising. Print media and the Internet carry a mixture of display and classified advertising. This is an important distinction. First, because approximately 40% of print media's advertising revenue comes from classifieds (though much of this is migrating to the Internet, a key medium for classified advertising). But second, and more importantly, grasping the different ways in which classified and display advertisements work is crucial to an understanding of how advertising works. Put simply, there are advertisements which people look for (classifieds), and advertisements which look for people (display). Display advertisements are necessarily intrusive, because they must catch the attention of people not initially interested in their messages; classified advertisements are not intrusive, because they rely on people perusing them for items they are consciously searching for.

Television, radio, posters, and cinema are, by their very nature as media, unsuitable for classified advertising (though 'Teletext' is a subcategory of classified). This partly explains why the arrival of television in the 1950s did not decimate print media in the way many people had predicted: the print media were buoyed up by the revenue from their classifieds. Equally, it is because the Internet is so especially good as a search medium that it has seriously bitten into the classified advertising revenues of print media in the 21st century.

Most mass media would not exist if they did not receive hefty revenues from advertising. The only exceptions are public service media like the BBC, wholly funded by the state, and paid for by governments in various ways around the world. These government-funded media comprise but a small fraction of the total international media scene. Nonetheless, media that depend on advertising funding, the vast majority of media, do not think of themselves as being part of the 'advertising industry' either. They see themselves as purveyors of news, information, and entertainment. They carry advertisements to subsidize all this, so they can provide cheap or even free media services. Within most media, there is a rigorous separation between the advertising and the editorial operations, and this is the way the editorial people (and probably the public) prefer it. So that although the advertisers and the media are far and away the largest sectors of the advertising tripartite, for neither of them is advertising 'their industry'.

The third leg of the advertising tripartite is the sector that produces the advertising campaigns: the advertising agencies. Advertising agencies create the advertisements, and on behalf of their clients they buy the space and time in the media, where the advertisements appear. The agencies are much the smallest sector of the advertising tripartite, but are the only sector that wholly relies on advertising for their living. It is this sector most people think of when they talk about people who work 'in advertising'. Certainly everyone who works in an agency (unlike those who work for an advertiser or for the media) will say they work in advertising. In the UK, agencies employ about 20,000 people – far fewer than are employed by advertisers, or by the media. The same is true, proportionately, in every country.

Until the 1970s, agencies did much more than just create advertisements and buy media for their clients. They handled almost every aspect of their clients' marketing communications. They employed far more people than they do today, and because they did many different things, they were called 'full-service' agencies. But during the 1970s things changed completely.

The demise of full-service agencies

As their name implies, from their inception advertising agents were paid commission by the media for bringing them business. But this commission level varied, and was highly competitive. Publications that found it hard to get advertising might pay agents as much as 30% for bringing them business; other agents, operating in better established areas, might be paid as little as 2% or 3%. Before 1914, the R. F. White agency handled all British government advertising for just 2½% commission. But the most common level of commission hovered around 15%.

During the first half of the 20th century, in almost all countries, the 15% commission level became the standard fixed rate of payment for agencies. In return for this fairly generous commission level, agencies were required by the media to be principals-at-law, legally responsible for paying the media even when their clients defaulted. Agencies were not permitted to rebate any part of the commission to their clients, and agencies were responsible for creating and delivering to the media their clients' advertisements. Agencies only received 15% commission if they were 'recognized' by the media, and agreed to the media's terms of business. In practice, the 15% commission system was a fixed-price closed shop. Though it was not surreptitious, and certainly not then illegal, the entire system was, in a way, a genteel conspiracy to rip off the advertisers. And in most countries it held supreme for more than half a century, moulding and shaping the structure of advertising agencies, and of the advertising industry, until the late 1970s.

Forbidden by the media to rebate commissions to their clients, agencies could not compete with each other on price, and so competed by offering their clients more and more ancillary services (not to mention generous entertainments). By the 1920s, creative and media-buying services were universally accepted as core advertising agency activities. But agencies then began to offer their clients an abundance of additional services which were not intrinsically advertising at all (though most of them were forms of marketing communication). Hence 'recognized' agencies became known, and liked to be known, as 'full-service' – they provided all the marketing services a client could want.

Though it is unlikely any one agency would have provided all of these at any one time, the raft of services advertising agencies then offered included:

- direct mail marketing
- door-to-door distribution
- home economist consultants
- in-store merchandising
- market research
- new product development
- package design
- poster site inspection
- product sample distribution
- public and press relations
- sales conference organization
- sales promotion
- trade exhibitions

Recognized agencies provided these and other services to their clients at cut prices: the agencies viewed them as loss-leaders, designed to help them hold on to their clients' business rather than to make additional profit. This was possible because the agencies were already making fat profits from their 15% commissions, which not only covered the cost of creating advertisements and buying media space, it subsidized the cost of these additional marketing services. But all this could not last. Two new developments cracked the cosy traditional system.

First, and in the long run most fundamentally, the leading specialists who worked in agencies and supplied most of the marketing services listed above broke away and set up their own specialist companies. Within agencies they had always been patronized, looked down upon by the advertising specialists, who correctly felt that they themselves were the agencies' *raison d'être*. But as new forms of marketing communication grew both in size and in complexity, the specialists who were really good at them left and launched their own businesses, to which many clients quickly gravitated. And agencies could not compete because they had long offered such services to their clients as loss-leaders, at cut prices, and their clients were unwilling to pay them more. Doubly unwilling when they realized the best practitioners of these services were leaving the advertising agencies to set up on their own.

Unlike the other marketing services, media buying had not been a loss-leader. Media buying had always been a core agency service. Nonetheless, the people who worked in media buying were, like the marketing services people, patronized by the advertising creative people, and were paid far less than the creative people. They did not like it. Media buying too was becoming big business, complex and highly specialized. So in the 1980s the best media buyers also broke away from the 'full-service' agencies and set up their own specialist shops. And again – initially with some hesitation – many clients followed them.

Second, at the same time governments, particularly in the UK and Europe, began to view the traditional 15% fixed-rate commission system as unacceptably anti-competitive. In Britain in 1976, the Office of Fair Trading ruled that the agency recognition and 15% commission system run by the media was in restraint of trade: illegal. The fixed-rate commission system swiftly disintegrated, and the 'full-service' agencies swiftly disintegrated with it, splitting into their constituent parts. Today almost all the old full-service agency functions are handled by specialist companies. Today the agencies which create and produce advertisements do little else, and are always called 'creative agencies'. The specialists who do little but plan and buy media are called 'media agencies'. Both types of agency are supported by 'planners', who help them carry out their roles. But even the planners are specialists.

Paradoxically perhaps, these developments have not been nearly so thoroughgoing in small agencies which work for small advertisers. Many of these smaller agencies are still 'full service', because they can only operate profitably by providing a bundle of services to their small clients, and their clients do not wish to pay the high fees the specialists charge.

And simultaneously a new animal has appeared in the advertising jungle: the marketing services conglomerate. These are generally mammoth, international holding companies. They own 'creative agencies' and 'media agencies', and numerous other types of marketing communications company – market research, public relations, package design, conference organization, marketing consultancy, and so on – throughout the world. And they keep all the different specialists in separate silos. The six largest holding companies, each of which employs tens of thousands of staff around the globe, are currently Omnicom (USA), WPP (UK), Interpublic (USA), Publicis (France), Dentsu (Japan), and Havas (France). These companies are often called 'advertising agencies'. This is a complete misnomer. Advertising is only one of the many marketing services their numerous subsidiaries provide, and nowadays rarely the dominant one.

The digital revolution

It might be thought that the separation of creative and media agencies would have converted the advertising tripartite into an advertising quadrapartite: advertisers, media, creative agencies, and media agencies. But while these changes were still being digested, at the end of the 20th century a completely new dynamic entered the advertising world: digital – and particularly Internet – advertising.

Throughout the world, the Internet has swiftly become a major advertising medium. Global Internet advertising expenditure has rocketed from $9 billion in 2002 to approximately $70 billion by 2011. This has provided both the creative and the media agencies with new opportunities – and new headaches. Neither the creation of Internet advertisements, nor the buying of space on the Internet, are done in quite the same ways creativity and media buying were done in the past. Agencies and clients have responded in two opposing ways. On the one hand, highly specialized new digital agencies have been launched; on the other

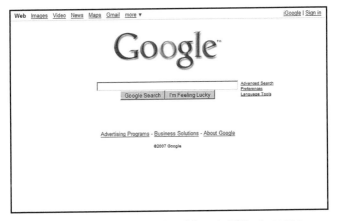

6. Global Internet advertising rocketed from $9 billion in 2002 to approximately $70 billion by 2011

hand, many established creative agencies and media agencies have set up digital 'departments', often as subsidiary companies, to handle their clients' digital advertising requirements. The jury is still out on whether digital advertising is best handled completely independently, by its own specialists, or best handled within established agencies, where it can be more easily integrated.

The old 15% commission and recognition structure had given the media disproportionate power in the advertising process. Though agencies were appointed by advertisers to handle their advertising, the agencies could not trade unless they were 'recognized' by the media. They had to face both ways, answering to both advertisers and media. Today all the different types of agency are paid directly by advertisers. The advertisers negotiate their fees, almost always based on the agency's time costs, determined by time sheets completed by agency staff. The fee negotiations are increasingly handled by the advertisers' purchasing departments: advertising and marketing services are bought like any other commodity. As mentioned, in total their fees approximate to around 10% of the advertisers' expenditure, a hefty saving of one-third against the old 15%. But, it must be remembered, advertisers buy all their other marketing communications services from other independent specialists. It seems most unlikely that they save money, overall.

The large marketing communications conglomerates, like WPP and Omnicom, try to sell to their clients bundles of the different services they provide. Their clients rarely buy into this proposition. They prefer to choose and appoint all their marketing communications suppliers independently and separately. The clients then require them all to work together, to maximize the effectiveness of their campaigns. Sometimes lines get crossed, and the various independent companies do not work together all that well. But there is no confusion about who is in charge of the show: the advertisers write the cheques, and they crack the whip. So we must now turn to the advertisers, and analyse them and the ways in which they operate in more detail.

Chapter 3
Advertisers: the paymasters

Why do advertisers advertise?

The first and most important decision any advertiser makes is…to advertise. Many people think large companies have no choice but to advertise. This is simply wrong. Many of the world's largest businesses – especially heavy industrial businesses like steel manufacturers or shipbuilders – do no advertising at all, or so little it hardly counts. They normally have no need to communicate with the public at large, and they have so few key customers they can reach them personally. Some other large companies, of which Google is perhaps the most famous example, get their name and what they offer across to the public in other ways than by advertising, usually 'word of mouth' recommendation. Nowadays this is often called 'viral marketing'. Viral marketing tends to be most successful when a business is relatively young and newsworthy: even Google had to start to advertise, using traditional media, in 2009. (Similarly, Virgin did little advertising in its early days, but is now a big advertising spender.)

Other businesses do not advertise themselves because they have no need to, but do advertise their output – movie companies and book publishers are good examples. With a few exceptions, the public neither knows nor cares which movie company made a particular movie or which publisher published a particular book:

they only want to know about the content of the film or book, and the writers, stars, and film directors involved.

Moreover, most members of the public believe – you may well yourself believe – that they are rarely, if ever, influenced by advertising. So if some companies succeed without advertising, and most people feel they are not influenced by advertising, why on earth do advertisers advertise?

Advertising costs money, and no business likes to spend money unless it has to. The businesses in the paragraph above know they do not have to spend money on advertising, so they don't. The businesses that do advertise – that is, the great majority of large businesses – believe that it is essential for them to do so. They believe, indeed they are convinced, that the benefits they obtain from advertising outweigh the costs, hopefully by a substantial margin. Which, then, are the businesses that advertise? On page 33 is a breakdown of the top dozen advertising sectors in Britain.

Though there will be national variations, this list will be much the same in almost all economically advanced countries – and for the same reasons. These business sectors have very large target markets, and they believe advertising to be the most cost-effective way to reach these target markets. Despite its considerable cost, they believe advertising is the least expensive means of persuading their target markets to buy their products. What is the basis for these seemingly optimistic beliefs?

If you have read much about advertising, you will probably have come across this maxim:

> I know half of all the money I spend on advertising is wasted, but I have no means of knowing which half.

In Britain, this maxim is usually attributed to the first Lord Leverhulme, the founder of Unilever; in America, it is attributed

Sector	Advertising expenditure (£millions)
Retailers	£2,257
Finance companies	£1,427
Entertainment, media, and leisure	£1,290
Fast-moving consumer goods	£1,086
Technological goods	£ 874
Automotive	£ 794
Toiletries/Cosmetics	£ 679
Travel and tourism	£ 663
Pharmaceutical	£ 404
Government and utilities	£ 357
Education and charities	£ 328
Electrical and household	£ 140

to the great retailer Sam Wanamaker. In fact, there is no evidence either of them said it. It is probably a bastardization of something rather similar said in 1916 by Adolph S. Koch, then the publisher of *The New York Times*. The maxim sounds profound and pregnant with meaning, which no doubt explains why it has survived for almost a century. But in reality it is, as soon as you begin to think about it, manifest tosh. What could it mean? That the first half of any television commercial is effective but the second half is not? That every alternate second is effective/ineffective/effective/ineffective...? That the left-hand side of every billboard works but the right-hand side is useless? The idea is incapable of analysis. However, the maxim does, tangentially, hint at a key aspect of advertising which is little understood.

Let us return to the notion of a 'Golden Key', which somehow makes some advertising successful while other advertising (lacking this notional Golden Key) is unsuccessful. Or as the maxim claims: there is advertising which is wasted, and advertising which is not wasted. The underlying assumption is that advertising is a game of two halves: advertising which works, and advertising which does not work. This belief is widespread, and is not confined to members of the public. It is almost universally accepted by people who work in advertising – whether they work for advertisers, the media, or agencies. But it is far, far too simple. Advertising is not a game of two halves; advertising is a rainbow, or anyway a prismatic spectrum.

Think of it this way. You want to sell an old bike. So you become an advertiser, and put an advertisement on the Internet or in your local paper's classified advertising section. You may get an offer from one prospective buyer, or two, or ten, or maybe even more than twenty – or from any number in between. Of course, you may get nil buyers, in which case you can argue the advertisement has definitely failed, though even here it may not be the advertisement as such that failed. Many people may have been interested by the advertisement but decided they didn't like the details of the bike mentioned: its colour, or its handlebars, or whatever. In any event, every level of response above nil shows *some* level of success, from minimal (one) to massive (20+). And anyway, few commercial advertisers ever run just a single advertisement. They run campaigns, with lots of advertisements. Almost inevitably, some of the advertisements generate some response, however small. Even some of the most celebrated disaster campaigns in advertising history, like those for Strand cigarettes in Britain and for the Ford Edsel car in America, sold a few cigarettes and a few cars. Advertising results, then, are not a black/white division into

An exciting new kind of car!

Makes history by making sense

Here's the car you hoped would happen. A full-size car that makes sense. Styled to last. Built to last. Beautifully efficient. And priced with the most popular three!

At last—a full-size car that makes sense. It looks right, works right. And it's priced right. The beautifully efficient Edsel for '59 is a car that slips easily into tight parking spaces—fits any normal garage. Same spacious room inside as before—*but less length outside!* It's a car that's powered to save. Edsel's four new engines include not only a thrifty six but a new economy V-8 that turns *regular* gas into spirited performance! It's a car that's distinctively styled to last. And carefully built to last. *Yet, the Edsel is actually priced with the most popular three!* See your Edsel Dealer. EDSEL DIVISION · FORD MOTOR COMPANY

7. One of the most celebrated campaign disasters in advertising history

success/failure, or wasted/not wasted. Advertising results are a continuum.

Moreover, for advertisers the key question is not merely whether the advertising generated any sales. The key question is: did the level of sales more than cover the cost of the campaign, and so produce a profit? Because this, or course, is why advertisers advertise: to make a profit.

Yet again, this is not an easy question to answer, because advertising generates – and advertisers almost always intend it to generate – both immediate sales and long-term sales. Advertisers want both to get back the money they have spent on their campaign fairly quickly and to build long-term brands. Advertisers want, as it were, to have their cake and eat it. So this is the final answer to why advertisers advertise: to realize a profit quite quickly – how quickly varies from advertiser to advertiser – and to make continuing profits in the future. And none of this is easy for advertisers to achieve, let alone easy to measure.

The IPA Advertising Effectiveness Awards

Over recent decades, as financial analysis techniques have grown ever more sophisticated in all aspects of business, questions of financial accountability have predictably grown ever more critical to advertisers. Top financial directors working for advertisers have grown increasingly powerful within their companies, and during the 1970s a new phrase – 'cost-effectiveness' – became the mantra of the day. The finance directors of major advertisers wanted their companies' advertising spends to be proved cost-effective, to show a proven profit on the company balance sheet.

Responding to their concerns, in the late 1970s a group of leading UK advertising agency researchers and planners, led by a man called Dr Simon Broadbent, realized it was becoming urgent for agencies to meet the challenge and prove how cost-effective advertising can be. Broadbent, with an Oxford first and a PhD from London University, had worked in Chicago after graduating, and he knew that advertising evaluation had made more progress in America than in Britain. In America, in 1961 the Association of National Advertisers – the advertisers, not the agencies – had published a highly influential short book called *Defining Advertising Goals for Measured Advertising Results* (DAGMAR). DAGMAR, which is still being regularly updated and republished, set out clear procedures for measuring advertising effectiveness, stressing that it was essential to specify in advance the measurement criteria, and the means of evaluation, to be used. All this remains equally true today. Following the publication of DAGMAR, in 1969 the American Marketing Association launched an awards competition called the EFFIES. The EFFIES awards were designed to honour campaigns that could *prove* they had been cost-effective.

Returning to Britain from America, Broadbent naturally knew all about DAGMAR and the EFFIES. He determined that Britain needed an advertising effectiveness awards competition of its own. By nature a somewhat academic business consultant rather than a words-and-pictures adman, Broadbent wanted the scheme to be more rigorous than the EFFIES. And he wanted it to be run by agencies rather than by advertisers. In 1980, he persuaded the British agencies' trade body, the Institute of Practitioners in Advertising (IPA), to launch the IPA Advertising Effectiveness Awards.

IPA Awards would be won only by the case histories of campaigns that showed detailed sales results, encoded for confidentiality if necessary. The papers entered would need to reveal exactly how the sales had been measured, and what market research had been carried out to validate them. (We will explore all this further in Chapter 7.) Every agency entry would have to be signed off by the advertiser, who would authenticate its accuracy. The case histories would be judged by a jury of eminent academics and business people, as well as by market researchers and leading agency people. In Broadbent's words, the creativity of the advertisements would play no part whatsoever in the competition. Indeed, rather surprisingly, the advertisements could not be part of the entry.

The IPA Awards had four aims: to persuade doubters and cynics that advertising is effective and measurable; to persuade advertisers – and especially advertisers' finance directors – that agencies are serious about sales and profitability, and don't care just about self-indulgent creativity, as is often suspected; to persuade agencies that producing cost-effective advertising can be good for their reputations; and to encourage best practice in campaign planning and evaluation. Over the succeeding three decades, those four aims have been achieved triumphantly.

Since 1980, some 1,000 case histories have been entered for the IPA Awards. In aggregate, they provide a rich databank of different brands and markets – large and small, national and regional, consumer and specialist. The 400 winning and commended papers are publicly available from the IPA databank, from the World Advertising Research Center website (http://www.warc.com), and in book form. Together they comprise the largest, most comprehensive, and most authoritative collection of successful advertising case histories available anywhere in the world. The IPA Awards do not prove that *all* advertising is cost-effective. As we saw in the preceding section, this is not true, nor could it ever be. But they demonstrate conclusively that well-planned advertising can be, and frequently is, extremely cost-effective.

Above all, the IPA papers have shown that advertising not only works, but works in a cornucopia of different ways. The list of advertisers' various possible campaign objectives that is shown on pages 5–6 is derived from them, as is the fact that the 'average' campaign has some 2.5 objectives. Though it was never their intention, the IPA Awards have demonstrated why no 'Golden Key' will ever be found – and they have proved that, although almost nobody admits they are influenced by advertising, whether they like it or not, they are!

Building profitable brands

Excellent as they were, the IPA Awards initially had a serious flaw. For the first decade, the entries concentrated on relatively short-term sales results, showing how well the advertising had worked over perhaps a couple of years. But as we saw earlier, advertisers generally want both short-term and long-term results. Advertisers want, and indeed need, their campaigns both to generate immediate sales and to build long-term brands.

Once again, it was Dr Simon Broadbent who identified this problem. In September 1988, he published an influential article in which he wrote: 'The IPA Awards should introduce a class of entries which is about the long-term … effects of advertising.' Two years later, in 1990, an appropriate new IPA Awards category was introduced. The first winner was PG Tips Tea. The winning paper was titled 'PG Tips' 35 Competitive Years at the Top of the Tea Market', and chronicled the story of the often hilarious, long-running PG chimps campaign, in which chimpanzees were endowed with human personalities and voices, and swigged down their PG tea with gusto. Since then, other successful long-term campaigns have been an integral part of the IPA Awards.

For advertisers, the embodiment of long-term sales is the *brand*. Brands first appeared in Victorian times, and numerous Victorian brands still exist after 200 years or more – that truly is long-term sales success! Bovril, Cadbury, Colman's, Crosse and Blackwell, Lea & Perrins, Oxo, Rowntree, Schweppes, *The Times*, and Wright's Coal Tar soap, to mention but a handful, are among the British brands that have achieved double-century longevity. Many of these brands recognized the importance of advertising from the start, and by the

8. The chimps helped make PG Tips the brand leader in the tea market for 35 years

1890s most were employing advertising agencies. In that decade, Pears Soap routinely spent over £100,000 annually on advertising, its budget having grown by leaps and bounds from a mere £80 in 1875. Frances Pears, the chairman of the family business, resigned as he was petrified that such huge advertising expenditures would bankrupt the company. Instead, the advertising built one of the first great soap brands.

9. Some leading brands have existed for over 200 years

What, then, is a brand? Brands and branding started out as a way
for manufacturers to help customers recognize their products, and
to buy them because they were consistent and reliable in an era of
adulterated goods and uneven quality control. However, today the
concept of a brand has become far more complex than that. Today
there must be almost as many definitions as there are brands in

the world. However, all agree that a brand, or anyway a successful brand, must meet the following four criteria:

1) The brand will have a unique name and packaging, and usually a logo, all of which will be easily and instantly recognizable by its target market.

2) It must be perceived by its target market to have qualities which differentiate it from other, similar brands. (This is called its *brand positioning*: these qualities define its position relative to other brands in its market.)

3) The qualities will be both functional and emotive: its purchasers will both think and feel the brand is different from, and in their eyes superior to, others.

4) These perceptions will allow the brand to command a premium price above *unbranded*, commodity products, and thus to generate greater profits for the company that owns it.

Brands do not necessarily need to be more expensive than their competitors: today retailers' own brands are usually cheaper, but are seen by their purchasers to be excellent value, that is the way such brands are superior. Brands do not necessarily need to be superior in quality to their competitors: in terms of quality, popular family cars cannot compete with Porsches and Bentleys, but again they are seen by their purchasers to be excellent value, and that is the way they are superior.

Clearly the concept of value is intrinsic to the concept of a brand. This is because value, like beauty, is in the eye of the beholder. It is the qualities that are valued by the brand's present and future customers – its target market – which matter. These may or may not be the qualities the technicians in the laboratories believe matter; they may or may not be the qualities that experts and pundits believe matter. It is the target market that chooses what matters, and what it is willing to pay for. Its choices will be influenced by experience of the product (or service); by the advertising; by other marketing communications; by media publicity of all kinds; and by personal recommendations. If these blend together to give the brand a strong and positive reputation – a strong and positive brand image (page 12) – the brand is destined for success. Perception, reputation, *image* are the essence of a brand. They are the reasons people buy (or do not buy) the brand. And more crucially, they are the reasons people continue (or do not continue) to buy the brand again and again.

If a brand's reputation, its image, is sufficiently strong, its success may continue for decades, or even, as we have just seen, for centuries. But this will only occur if the brand owner – the advertiser – continuously nurtures the brand, ensuring that it constantly and unremittingly offers good value to its target market. In the fast- changing and highly competitive world in which we live, this will not occur by happenstance. It will demand persistent effort and careful management, continuing brand development and improvement. But all this is well worth the effort. Brands can be the keystones upon which the long-term success of companies is built. Brands ensure that the profits made by advertising campaigns are not fly-by-night: the campaigns deliver profits almost immediately and profits in the future – exactly what advertisers require in order to build healthy long-term businesses.

One final point on the subject of branding. Nowadays brands are so important that most advertising people, both in and out of agencies, talk as though all advertising is brand advertising, designed to produce long-term as well as short-term results. Though this is generally the case, it is not universally true. Think again of that old bike advertisement (page 34). Once the bike is sold, that's it: job done. Similarly, a fair amount of direct response advertising, selling goods directly from the page or off the screen, is instant, and not really branded. Customers respond to each individual advertisement, and other customers may respond to the next one. The companies who run such advertising will, if they are good at their business, go on and on, running offer after offer. But they may not bother, or want, to build themselves as brands. They have no need to.

This is another telling example of how varied and disparate advertising can be. In the great advertising firmament, however, such advertisers occupy but a tiny niche. Brands are the stars and galaxies which glitter and gleam throughout advertising's skies.

Chapter 4

The media: blowing the advertisers' trumpets

The media spectrum

We now come to the second part of the advertising tripartite: the media that carry the advertisements. Once again, we must begin by carefully defining what the *media* are, especially because 'media' has become something of a jargon word in recent times, much abused and misused. During the last 100 years or so, both the number and the variety of media have exploded. A wide spectrum of totally new media have arrived, and older media have divided and subdivided themselves to reach ever more specific groups, in carefully targeted ways. And with the more recent arrival of the Internet and of digitization, the entire advertising media scene has found itself in a state of considerable flux. Since the beginning of the 21st century, media throughout the world have been constantly changing. It is almost anybody's guess where these changes will eventually end up (and almost everybody in the media is willing to offer a guess or two). The best that can be done here, therefore, is to give a clear picture of the media as they are today, with some hints as to what the future may bring.

Media is, of course, simply the Latin plural form of the singular noun *medium*. *Medium* has several overlapping meanings, but in the *Oxford English Dictionary* you will find the relevant definition to be:

Any intervening substance through which a force acts on objects at a distance or through which impressions are conveyed to the senses.

This almost exactly defines what a medium is in advertising: 'Any intervening substance...through which impressions are conveyed to the senses.' The impressions are the advertisements, and the leading media conveying them to our senses are the newspapers, magazines, television, radio, direct mail, posters and transport, cinema, and the Internet.

Naturally, advertisers have to pay the media for conveying their messages. And this leads us to the three basic criteria by which advertisers judge the effectiveness of all advertising media:

1) How many people in the advertiser's target market does the medium reach? And – using market research – what kind of people are they?
2) How much does it cost to use the medium? (And compared with alternative media, is it the best possible value for money?)
3) How powerful and persuasive is it as an advertising medium – particularly for the specific goods or services being advertised?

In this chapter, we will mainly be looking at advertising media in the UK. But these three questions are fundamental to all advertising media, around the globe. To explore them we will now consider each of the main UK advertising media sectors, looking first at their relative sizes, as measured by the amounts of advertising money spent with each of them. Their relative sizes vary from country to country, but these key media, often called the 'prime media' in advertising, are important everywhere.

It will readily be seen that in little more than a decade, the Internet has won a massive share of the advertising market in the UK – as it has in every country in the world. Most of its gains have come in the form of 'search' advertising – where you click-through from sponsored listings to promotional websites. Internet search

Share of UK advertising expenditure by media

	Share of expenditure (%)
Press and magazines	31%
Television	24%
Direct mail	12%
Outdoor and transport	5%
Radio	3%
Cinema	1%
Internet	24%
TOTAL	100%

advertising is akin to traditional classified advertising, and the Internet has gained most of its search advertising at the expense of newspaper and magazine classified advertising sections. But Internet display advertising – banners, pop-ups, and the like – has also steadily gained display revenue from the traditional media, though not to anything like the same extent as 'search' has done. Even after more than a decade's existence, nobody can tell how large the Internet's share of advertising will eventually grow to become, nor, by implication, how hard the traditional media will eventually be hit. But the general consensus is that the Internet's advertising growth will continue for many years yet.

Having said which, the longer established media still receive more than 80% of all advertising expenditure, and so it is these that we will consider first.

Press and magazines

Contrary to most people's perceptions, with 31% of all revenue, print media are still the biggest media sector. The money spent in press and magazines breaks down:

National newspapers

With 11 major national dailies and the same number of national Sundays, Britain has the strongest and most diverse national press in the world:

	Share of expenditure (%)
National newspapers (including supplements)	27%
Regional newspapers (including free sheets)	30%
Consumer magazines	11%
Trade and professional journals	9%
Directories	13%
All other	10%
TOTAL	100%

National dailies (read by 44% of the UK adult population in total)

Daily Express
Daily Mail
Daily Mirror
Daily Record (Scotland)
Daily Star
Daily Telegraph
Financial Times
The Guardian
The Independent
The Sun
The Times

National Sundays (read by 48% of the UK adult population in total)

Independent on Sunday
Mail on Sunday
News of the World
People
Sunday Express
Sunday Mail (Scotland)
Sunday Post (Scotland)
Sunday Telegraph
Sunday Times
The Observer

This galaxy of national newspapers provides advertisers with
a plethora of choice unparalleled in other countries. The UK
circulations of these papers varies from the largest, the *News
of the World* (3,087,000) down to the smallest, the *Financial
Times* (134,000). Nowadays market research data (like the Target
Group Index, see page 10) provides a vast amount of information
about the readers of each newspaper. Advertisers can thus select
for their campaigns the papers that are specifically read by their
target markets. The cost of buying advertising space is broadly

proportional to the size of the circulation, but the quality papers – such as the *Financial Times* and *The Times*, the *Sunday Times* and *Sunday Telegraph* – can charge higher prices because they provide advertisers with more affluent and more influential readers. And because a significant proportion of advertisers want their campaigns to reach affluent and influential people, they are willing to pay a premium price to advertise in the papers these people read.

The cost of the advertising will also be determined by the size of the advertisement, whether or not it is in colour, and its whereabouts in the newspaper. Larger advertisements cost more than smaller ones, but the cost is not directly proportional to size: to encourage advertisers to buy bigger spaces, smaller advertisements are generally slightly more expensive *pro rata*. Colour advertisements are more expensive than black and white ones: historically, this was because colour used to cost more to print – today the printing cost differentials are small, and the price differentials simply reflect supply and demand. Similarly, newspapers charge more for advertisements in certain positions, positions which many advertisers want because they are looked at by more readers of the publication, or by their particular target market (sports products on sports pages, for example); obviously the cost of printing the advertisements does not change with the position – again, the different prices simply reflect supply and demand.

With so many newspapers to choose from, and so much choice within each newspaper, the buying and selling of space in newspapers is extremely flexible, and subject to considerable negotiation. For the advertiser, the key factor in making the final selection will be the *cost per thousand readers*. This figure is the cost of the chosen space – large or small, colour or monochrome, wherever positioned – per 1,000 readers in the advertiser's target market. Media buying specialists will calculate exactly how much it costs to reach this notional 1,000 target readers in all the available newspapers. They will then be able to make an objective cost comparison between all the possibilities, and unless there are special circumstances, the media specialist will advise the advertiser to place their campaign in the cheapest newspaper or newspapers.

This *cost per thousand* calculation, suitably adjusted, applies in all media – whether it be cost per thousand readers, or television viewers, or radio listeners, or (in the case of direct mail) addressees. It is seldom a helpful device when making comparisons *between* media: you cannot sensibly compare the cost per thousand for a television commercial with the cost per thousand for a magazine advertisement – the effects of the different media are too disparate. But within any one media sector, cost per thousand is the single most potent weapon in the media buyer's armoury. Provided you minimize the cost of reaching your target market, as an advertiser you won't go far wrong.

Regional newspapers

In the USA and many other countries, where there are very few national newspapers and their circulations are quite small, regional newspapers are even more important as advertising media than they are in Britain. However, even in Britain, there are over 1,100 regional newspapers and, as can be seen above, to many people's surprise they carry more advertising than the national newspapers. This is because they are, in total, read by significant numbers of the population.

Most of the regionals' advertising revenue comes from national retailers and local advertisers. With the exception of retailers, national advertisers rarely advertise in regional papers. This is because the cost per thousand in regionals is far higher than it is in the nationals. The cost per thousand circulation of a full-page advertisement (black and white) is six times higher in the regional

	Percentage of UK adults who read
Regional weeklies (free)	44%
Regional weeklies (paid)	24%
Regional mornings and evenings	15%
Regional Sundays	5%

Bristol Evening Post than in the national *Sun*, for example. Other regional versus national newspaper comparisons would be similar. This is why, in the UK, national advertisers almost always use national newspapers, *except* when there is a specific reason to advertise locally.

While, as has been said, comparing costs per thousand between different media sectors can be unreliable – to some degree, you will always be comparing apples with oranges – it is nonetheless important to know that the cost per thousand is nowadays often cheaper for Internet advertising than it is for newspapers. This is a key reason why so much advertising expenditure is migrating from newspapers to the Internet. In both the UK and the USA, the previously strong network of regional newspapers is under severe competitive threat from the Internet, and in consequence the long-term future of regional newspapers is, at present, far from assured.

Consumer magazines

For advertisers, consumer magazines can broadly be divided into two groups:

- General interest and women's magazines
- Special interest and hobby magazines

As might be expected, the first group have relatively high readership levels, just below those of the national press.

	Percentage of UK adults who read
Any general weekly	33%
Any general monthly	40%
Any woman's weekly	21%
Any woman's monthly	35%

The readerships of special interest and hobby magazines are far smaller. So most of the major national advertisers who use magazines for their campaigns use general magazines – such as the *Radio Times* (circulation 1,046,726) – or women's magazines – such as *Good Housekeeping* (circulation 430,971). Special interest and hobby magazines' circulations usually fall in the 50,000 to 100,000 bracket. Moreover, although their advertising rates are relatively low, as with regional newspapers their costs per thousand circulation are relatively high – almost always exceeding those of the general and women's magazines. Still, for advertisers whose target markets are specific – minority sectors of the population, like anglers or amateur photographers – specialist magazines are ideal, and they are able to sell space at a premium price to advertisers aiming at those very specific, relatively small markets.

As with newspapers, magazines charge more for larger than for smaller advertising spaces, more for colour than for black and white, and more for specially prized positions: at the front of the magazine or facing editorial articles, for example. However, one important advantage magazines have over newspapers is that they lie around far longer (think of the ancient issues you sometimes find in dentists' waiting rooms!). This longevity means they accumulate far more *readers per copy* than newspapers do. As a result, their readerships are far higher than their circulation numbers suggest. Readership data from market research surveys shows that *Vogue*, for example, has some 6 readers per copy, while *Golf World* has a massive 12.5 readers per copy. No newspaper has that many readers per copy. And as advertisers are generally more interested in total readership numbers than in simple circulation numbers, the *cost per thousand readers*, as well as the *cost per thousand circulation*, will be an important factor influencing the choice of which newspapers and magazines to use for any campaign.

Trade journals and directories

The two remaining major groups of publications in the print sector, trade and professional journals and directories, together carry some 22% of all print advertising expenditure – so are larger than the consumer magazine sector, though the latter has a much higher profile for major advertisers.

The reason for their low profile is that neither trade and professional journals, nor directories, are seen as general advertising media. Their roles are far more specific. As with specialist and hobby magazines, they are ideal for reaching their particular target markets. Trade and professional journals will therefore be used extensively by advertisers wishing to reach, for example, doctors or dentists, builders or engineers. There are some 2,000 trade and professional journals in the UK, covering almost every trade and professional sector you can think of, with circulations usually in the 20,000 to 50,000 bracket.

Directories, in contrast, have massive circulations, and even larger readerships. Over 30 million people in the UK consult *Yellow Pages* annually. But the vast majority of advertisements in directories are 'listings' – and listings are like newspaper classifieds: advertisements which people look for, rather than advertisements which look for people. They do not therefore involve advertising skills in the same way that display advertisements do. However, it must not be forgotten that there are also a fair number of display advertisements in directories, some of them from major national advertisers – and these call for much the same skill and input as display advertisements in other printed media.

We have now completed our analysis of printed advertising media. It is time to take a look at television.

Television

In the public mind, throughout the world, television is the archetypical and predominant advertising medium. Indeed, when members of the public are asked where they have seen any advertisement, the likelihood is they will say they saw it on television – even if the advertisement has never appeared on television. (A perfect illustration of the fallibility of people's memories, and a warning that market research results must always be interpreted with caution.)

Commercial television – television funded by advertising – started in the USA in the 1930s, but did not begin in Britain until 1955, and in Britain it was thought from the start to be so powerful that it needed to be controlled by parliamentary statute. While other media are permitted to publish as much advertising as they wish (though poster sites are controlled by local authorities), the 1954 Act which set up British commercial television ensured that the quantity, timing, and content of advertisements would be controlled by statutory bodies. Not until December 2003 did

Ofcom – the governmental regulator now responsible for British commercial television – subcontract control of the *content* of television advertisements. However, Ofcom retained control of the quantity of advertising, and of its overall timing.

The consequences of this government control have been considerable, and are entirely foreign to other media in the UK – though television advertising is subject to similar constraints in many countries of the world (excluding the USA). In the UK, the limit on the number of minutes that can be devoted to advertisements in any hour has influenced the cost of television advertising; the control of the content of television advertisements has made it necessary for all commercials to be approved before they are transmitted, both in script form and when finally produced (unlike advertisements in other media); the control of the timing of advertising has allowed the government to ensure that commercials for certain products will not be transmitted at times it deems inappropriate (mainly, this means that commercials it is felt children ought not to see must not be transmitted until late in the evening).

Initially, the UK government sought to build up a regional television broadcasting structure by assigning separate contracts to different regional companies, each of which – like a local newspaper – covered its own allotted area of the UK. This system worked well at first. But from the 1960s onwards, a raft of additional commercial channels were launched – first Channel 4, then 5, GMTV, Sky, and a host of other satellite broadcasters – at which point the old regional structure became hopelessly blurred. Today over 600 terrestrial, satellite, and cable television stations broadcast in the UK, the great majority of them reaching tiny, specialized viewing audiences but covering the entire country. All must be licensed to broadcast by Ofcom, and pay Ofcom a fee for their licence.

However, the largest television audiences still gravitate towards the long-established terrestrial stations. This occurs even in the 40% of UK homes that receive both terrestrial and satellite channels:

Terrestrial

BBC1	21%
BBC2	7%
ITV 1	18%
Channel 4	7%
Five	5%
TOTAL TERRESTRIAL	58%

Satellite

SKY (all)	4%
ITV 2, 3, 4	4%
BBC 3, 4	2%
Others (none exceeds 1%)	32%
TOTAL SATELLITE	42%

The media: blowing the advertisers' trumpets

The fragmentation of television audiences during recent decades, which has happened throughout the globe as new channels have been launched everywhere, has caused advertisers much concern. Advertisers look back nostalgically to the years when a single spot transmission would be seen by the majority of the population at one fell swoop. (This was true even in the USA, where there have always been far more channels than in European countries.) This made the television advertising of mass consumer products relatively straightforward – not to say easy – whereas today it is necessary for advertisers to build up coverage of their target markets over time, by advertising on a host of channels with separate audiences. Still, it is arguable that advertisers worry rather too much about this problem, as advertising in other media has always been fragmented. Moreover, advertisers gain considerable benefits from the price competition between the numerous broadcasting stations. And television remains much the fastest way to build up public awareness of a new brand or a new campaign. Seldom does a new brand or new campaign that solely uses other media, without using television, reach high levels of public awareness very quickly.

Television is also the most thoroughly researched of all the media. In the UK, viewership data is provided by the Broadcasters' Advertising Research Board Limited (BARB), a company set up by the advertising industry to provide robust and trustworthy information to all interested parties. BARB subcontracts the collection of this information to several research companies. The most basic data is collected from a sample of 5,100 homes, in all of which meters are connected to their television sets. These meters record continuously whether or not the set is on, which channel it is tuned to, and when channels are changed. These 5,100 homes represent some 11,300 residents. An additional 52,500 individual viewers are interviewed annually, and their viewership data correlated with the 5,100 meter records. Viewership results from the meters are published on a minute-by-minute basis, and the data is processed overnight to be released at 9.30am the following morning.

As with other media, the key tool in the advertiser's television time-buying toolbox is the *cost per thousand target viewers*. The BARB research system means that in many ways the buying of television advertising time is both more accurate and more complex than the buying of time in print media, because far more is known about the ways viewers watch than is known about reading patterns. The exact composition of television audiences, broken down by age, sex, employment, region, family composition, buying habits, and other data, can be continuously analysed. For example, viewers' programme switching can be tracked throughout an evening; and the different viewing patterns in houses with multiple sets can likewise be measured. All this makes it possible to pinpoint the television viewing of target markets with great accuracy. The media buyer will then be able to evaluate precisely, on a cost per thousand basis, which programmes, and even which breaks in which programmes, will reach the target market most cost-effectively. There are great differences in price, for example, between *peak-time* (mid-evening) and *off-peak* (early, late, and daytime) spots, and the differences approximately reflect the size and composition of the audiences.

Still, it must not be thought that all this makes the buying of television advertising robotic. Viewers often fail to watch programmes they have been predicted to watch, and inter-channel competition can make audience levels unpredictable. Nonetheless, television time buying is probably the most sophisticated system of mass media advertising buying, the world over.

Before leaving television, two myths need to be dispelled. First, it is widely believed that the advent of the Internet has resulted in television viewership falling. There is no evidence of this happening; on the contrary, though fragmentation has meant that each individual channel's viewership has fallen, total television viewing – in terms of number of hours per week – continues to increase, steadily if slowly. Second, it is widely believed that the advent of Video-on-Demand, and the use of zappers, results in people zapping through commercials, to the advertisers' disadvantage. Again, the evidence shows this to be the opposite of the truth – partly because V-o-D encourages people to watch more television, and partly because only a tiny minority of viewers zap through commercials, and then only occasionally. Despite the increasing competition in all media, the future of television advertising seems assured.

Minor media

As can be seen from the table on page 47, excluding the Internet, the remaining media – direct mail, radio, outdoor and transport, and cinema – account for just 21% of total advertising expenditure between them, and so we must deal with them quite briefly. This is not to minimize their effectiveness as advertising media for many products, and for many target markets. Indeed, their strengths often lie in their specificity. But they generally lack the mass impact of the more major advertising media, which is why they tend to carry less advertising.

Direct mail

With its 12% share of total expenditure, direct mail is currently the fourth largest advertising medium in the UK. (It is a much larger advertising medium in the USA, mainly because of the dearth of strong national daily newspapers there. The mail is an inexpensive means of distributing advertising messages throughout the vast terrain.)

Before the arrival of the Internet, direct mail was the sole means of identifying individuals personally, and usually by name – and it remains a most effective 'personal' medium. This often makes it possible to communicate with specific target markets with great accuracy. Over the years, advertisers and companies that specialize in providing direct mail 'lists' have built up individualized lists of the users of many products. While a small proportion of the public complains about what they call 'junk mail', the reality is that the vast majority of the population accept it without objection, and often respond to it.

This is known, and can be evaluated, because direct mail is one of the most *measurable* media. Because it is so personalized, the response to most mailings can be, and is, exactly quantified. Costs and results can be compared, and cost-effective mailings can thus be virtually *guaranteed* to produce profitable business for the advertiser, which happens in no other medium – except, as we shall see, the Internet.

Outdoor and transport

Most people are surprised to learn that this sector – billboards, posters, public transport advertising, and the like – is as small as it is, with only 5% of total expenditure. The public feels it sees advertising hoardings everywhere – and this is true in the centres of most towns. But elsewhere there are relatively few hoardings, not least because the placement of outdoor advertising is strictly controlled by local authorities.

Posters can be placed with precision locally, and so are frequently used by local (rather than national) advertisers. Throughout history, posters have given designers and writers the opportunity to be wonderfully creative, and many of the campaigns which people remember for years start life on the hoardings. But since the arrival of commercial television over 50 years ago, outdoor advertising has come to be seen, unfairly, as a 'support' medium, a reminder medium, and is now only occasionally used as the principal medium for a major new campaign or product.

10. Most people are surprised billboards and posters have only a small share of the advertising market

Radio

Radio too tends to be seen as a support or reminder medium. Being another broadcast medium, it is also often seen, again unfairly, as 'cheap television'. This is wrong because – although radio is certainly a much cheaper advertising medium than television – it is not truly comparable. Television is quintessentially a visual medium: above all, people remember, and are influenced by, what they see. By definition, radio is not visual, and so requires a completely different creative approach, based on words and sounds. But used imaginatively, words and sounds can produce extremely effective advertising.

Radio audiences are also far smaller than television audiences, and much more locally focused. So radio can, like posters (and cinema), be used to great effect by local advertisers.

Cinema

Cinema is also frequently used as a support medium, another 'different form of television'. But cinema's great strength is that its audiences tend to be relatively young – and many advertisers see young consumers as their prime target market. Because cinema campaigns are generally aimed at the young, many cinema commercials are quite unlike television commercials, with film sequences specifically created with the young in mind (which sometimes baffle the older members of the audience).

The Internet

Though still thought of as being very new, in the UK the Internet first surfaced as an advertising medium in 1997, when it was registered as carrying £8 million worth of advertising. In that same year, Internet advertisements were for the first time judged separately at Britain's leading creative awards competition. However, in Britain, as everywhere else, the Internet's growth since then has been startling, with advertising revenue leaping from the £8 million in 1997 to more than £34 million in 2009 – 24% of total expenditure and still climbing rapidly. Most Internet advertising is for products and brands for which customers want quite detailed information: finance, telecommunications, computers, travel, automobiles, industrial goods, and entertainment are the top seven Internet advertising sectors. Inexpensive branded consumer goods account for only some 5% of Internet advertising.

In part, this is because the Internet has become the prime *interactive* medium. It allows, indeed encourages, customers to respond to advertisements by way of chat rooms and other online discussion forums, so that advertisers and customers engage directly in dialogue with each other. Internet enthusiasts often claim that this interactivity is revolutionizing marketing, as advertisers and their customers build increasingly close relationships. There is a smidgeon of truth in this, but traditional retailers have always been close to their customers – after all, the customers personally visit their shops – and anyway, the vast majority of customers do not respond to advertisers via the Internet, nor do they wish to.

However, online behaviours and interactivity differ greatly between different socioeconomic groups. Consequently the Internet is highly effective for targeting defined demographic groups, both by special interests and activities, and at different times during the day and night. For example, online behaviour differs markedly according to age, sex, and class. Urban professionals aged 20–34 rely on the Internet heavily for their work, and for planning their social lives. Women aged 35–44 with families, in contrast, use it to manage the home, and for hobbies and other interests. Moreover, Internet users can be identified, and their purchasing and other characteristics can be related directly to them, by means of the memories ('cookies') in their computers. This makes Internet targeting far more precise than that for any other medium.

We have now explored all the major advertising media in the UK – and thus, indirectly, in the world. Though the relative size and importance of each medium will change from country to country, as has been said, the fundamentals remain constant. The fundamentals are determined by the technical nature of each medium, and the human nature of consumers. These do not change.

Chapter 5
The creative agencies: creating new campaigns

We saw in Chapter 2 that since the end of the 20th century advertising agencies have become increasingly specialized. Before then, agencies provided their clients with a wide range of varied marketing services. From the 1970s onwards, with the breakdown of the 15% commission system, agencies began to focus on their two core competencies: creating advertisements and buying media. These two distinct activities soon came to be carried out by different specialist companies: creative agencies and media agencies. This organizational structure still pertains today, and so we will consider each of the two specializations separately, in this and the next chapter, starting with creative agencies.

First steps in creativity

Most people think advertisements are dreamed up when 'creative people' are told 'We need a new campaign for Boggins beer – get your skates on and be quick about it!' After which a creative person puts an ice pack on his or her head, sits in a dark room for a few hours until inspiration hits them, and then animatedly announces 'I've got it! – "There's No Better Beer than Boggins!"'

Well, not quite. While the sitting and thinking is roughly akin to a key part of the process, the rest of that little scenario is illusory in three essential ways. First, as has already been stated, the creative people will not start work without a written, detailed advertising strategy which has been agreed by their client, Boggins, and by the agency's senior management. Second, creative people almost never work individually nowadays, they always work in copy/art teams of two people. Third, at this initial stage the copy/art team will almost always have several ideas (usually called '*concepts*') which they will want to discuss with their colleagues before refining one or two of them (and they will rarely arrive at these concepts in just a few hours).

As was detailed at the beginning of this book, the advertising strategy document will include the campaign's objective(s); facts about the brand which show the objectives to be realistic; the brand's competitors, with details of their advertising and marketing campaigns; a summary of any relevant market research – saying why consumers use the brand, and why they do not; the message the campaign must communicate, and the tone in which it must be communicated; which media are likely to be used for the campaign; the budgets available both for the preparation of the advertisements and for the media campaign; a timescale for both the preparation of the advertisements and for the duration of the media campaign; any other details felt to be especially important in this instance; and, particularly, the target market at which the campaign will aim.

The creative team will need and want to know all this information. They will need to know the media likely to be used, so they don't create print advertisements when a television commercial is required. They will need to know the budget available, so they don't create advertisements which simply cannot be afforded. They will need to know how long they have to prepare the campaign. They will need to know the target market at which the campaign will aim, so they can keep it in their mind's eye all the time – and avoid creating messages suitable for impecunious teenagers when a campaign aimed at the affluent elderly is required. But for them, the absolutely vital part of the advertising strategy will be: the message the campaign must communicate, and the tone in which it must be communicated.

One of the most difficult lessons advertising creative people – and advertisers – have to learn is that the messages you put into advertisements are but the means to an end. The end is what the target market makes of the messages. It is not the messages you put *into* an advertisement that matter, it is the messages the target market takes *away* from the advertisement that matter. Most novitiate advertisers and creative people believe that if you say something in an advertisement, this is what people will take from it. Maybe, maybe not. Just as it is easy for people to misunderstand what they are told in conversation, it is doubly easy for them to misunderstand what they see and hear in advertisements. They generally pay little attention to advertisements, picking up only the broadest outline; they frequently focus on aspects of advertisements that were included only as unimportant props; they often forget most of the content of an advertisement, remembering only the bits that grabbed them. So it is essential not to overcrowd advertisements with too much information, a failing of many advertisers. Often, people can remember the advertisement but not remember which brand it was for. For all these reasons, the brief for the 'message that must be communicated', as defined in the advertising strategy, must be short, simple, unequivocal, and clear. And any ideas the creative team come up with must be checked rigorously against this brief.

But the message in an advertisement does not include only the words and pictures used. It includes the *way* they are used. The tone, the style, the personality of the advertisement. Exactly the same words, spoken in different tones of voice or set in different typefaces, will convey totally different messages. Here is a simple example. A party invitation in traditional embossed copperplate lettering on deckle-edged heavy card will lead the recipient to expect a totally different kind of party from an invitation – using exactly the same words – set in ghoulish, haunted-house lettering, printed in blood red on glittering foil. The message will be precisely the same: please come to my party. But the tone, the style, the personality of each will promise an utterly different event. In consequence, each will appeal to completely different types of people, different target markets – and turn others off. The same is true of advertisements. The actors, the models, the typefaces, the design, the props – every detail of the advertisement will contribute to its tone. And its tone must be calculated to appeal to its target market, otherwise the effectiveness of the message will inevitably be impaired. Consequently, advertising creative people must be exceptionally sensitive to the nuances of current styles, current fashions, current vernacular language. Naturally, the typefaces, the design – and even the models and props chosen – will principally be the province of an art director rather than a copywriter (though both will have their say); and the language will be principally the province of the copywriter rather than the art director (though again both will have their say). This is one of the reasons why advertising creative people nowadays always work in teams of two: copy and art together.

But this was not always the case. Until roughly the middle of the 20th century, all over the world, new advertisements were normally created by copywriters, working alone – rather like the Boggins beer copywriter in the scenario above. The copywriter would indeed put a metaphorical ice-pack on his head, and come up with the words and maybe a rough idea for the illustration. He – it was almost always a 'he' in those days – would then send his words and idea to a 'visualizer', somebody paid to visualize the copywriter's thoughts. The visualizers worked in a different department, often nowhere near the copywriters. The visualizers would be typographers, or sometimes graphic designers. But in this hierarchy the copywriter was top dog. The visualizer brought the copywriter's idea to life – but it was still the copywriter's idea. All this roughly made sense, because print advertising, then much the largest sector of advertising, was primarily verbal. The words were all-important.

Then came television. Television is essentially a visual medium – or a visual/verbal medium. Television advertising began in the USA in the 1930s, and by the 1940s American agencies were questioning the 'lone copywriter' approach to creativity. One agency in particular pioneered the copy/art team approach to creativity. This was a New York agency called Doyle Dane Bernbach (DDB). In the 1950s, DDB quickly built a reputation as the most highly creative agency around, first in America and then throughout the world. DDB famously recruited some of the most talented creative people in American advertising. And the copy/art team philosophy was central to its creativity, because this massively raised the status of the 'art' person – now given the title 'art director'. No longer did the visualizer simply interpret the copywriter's ideas: the copy/art team worked together, from the start.

Nor did the team work solely on television advertising. It was soon discovered that copy/art teams enhanced creativity in all media. And as the number and different types of media have burgeoned, this union of talents has grown ever more essential. Today almost all advertising campaigns have to be sufficiently adaptable to work in a host of media, from television to in-store shelf-cards, from posters to the Internet. Whatever the medium, the copywriter and the art director create ideas together, in tandem, each bringing their own different training and talents to the process. And advertisements have proved all the stronger for it. DDB's early campaigns – for Volkswagen, for EL AL, for Avis car rentals, and a galaxy of others – quickly became famous around the globe. A new kind of advertising had been born, in which advertisement concepts literally fused words and visuals. Advertisers flocked to DDB, and its business grew like wildfire.

Partly because commercial television did not start in Britain until 1955, and partly because the British advertising bosses were reluctant to adopt a new creative system they thought to be dangerously radical and expensive – the new 'art directors'

11. Bill Bernbach, who built DDB New York into the world's most highly creative agency in the 1960s

12. **DDB's VW campaign quickly became famous around the globe for its creativity**

demanded far higher salaries than the visualizers had been paid –
the copy/art team approach did not cross the Atlantic until the
early 1960s. It started at what was to become Britain's own leader
in creativity, the agency Collett Dickensen Pearce (CDP). CDP had
a close working relationship with DDB, and so knew all about its

creative 'team' system. CDP, like DDB before it, quickly gained a worldwide reputation for outstanding creativity. Its campaigns for Benson and Hedges, Heineken, Hamlet cigars, and many others scooped up awards at all the world's leading creative festivals. During the 1960s and early 1970s, these two agencies dominated world advertising creativity.

Today virtually all advertising creativity, in every leading agency in the world, is produced by copy/art teams. Generally, the copywriter and the art director form a long-term relationship, and move together from agency to agency whenever they change jobs. Obviously, as in all relationships, they occasionally split up and find new partners. But such splits are surprisingly rare. Creative people find it difficult to discover a mate with whom they can work well – and having discovered one, they try hard to keep their relationship alive.

How long will it take a creative team to come up with a new campaign idea? Well, how long is a piece of string? An idea may come almost instantly, or may take weeks in gestation. Will the team come up with just one idea, or with several, for further

13. CDP's Heineken campaign scooped up international creative awards

consideration? There can be no single answer to this. Sometimes the team has an idea it is absolutely sure is absolutely right. More often, the team will have a few ideas, all of which it feels could be developed with further time and thought. The team will then want to involve others in assessing the quality of its various ideas. It will discuss them with other creative colleagues, and at this point account planning – which we left at the end of Chapter 1 – may re-enter the creative process. But before we involve ourselves further in this process, it will be helpful, indeed necessary, to explore the nature of creativity, and of the creative people upon whom so much in advertising depends.

The nature of creativity

What is creativity? Even more than any of the other definitions we have considered, creativity is impossible to define with any accuracy – though many people have tried, and you will find many definitions in dictionaries. It is sometimes said that, although it cannot be defined, it can easily be recognized. Like lots of other things said about creativity, this is a half-truth. Yes, creativity can be recognized, but different people recognize different things as being creative. As we all know, most people at first rejected the Impressionists' paintings as not being art, while today they are accepted as being among the greatest works of art in history. The same has been true in music, and in literature. And it has sometimes happened in advertising.

The concept of creation – making something out of nothing, bringing things into existence for the first time – has fascinated and perplexed humanity throughout the ages. Almost throughout history it was generally accepted that creativity 'just happens'. Ideas float into the mind of their own accord, unpredictably, and no further explanation is possible. The most common cartoon depiction of this phenomenon is of an electric bulb suddenly lighting up, for no explicit reason, in the brain. But this is altogether too simple a view of creativity.

First, it suggests ideas come about without prior cogitation. But it would be hard to find a great creative thinker who did not say ideas are the result of long cogitation. Sir Isaac Newton did not simply discover gravity when he saw an apple falling, as the famous anecdote claims. He had been thinking about the nature of gravity for years. Indeed, when asked how he came by his discoveries, Newton replied 'By always thinking about them'. Yes, new ideas do come to highly creative people 'out of the blue'. But they come because creative people constantly seek them, both consciously and subconsciously.

Second, the light bulb image suggests that ideas arrive fully formed in the brain. This seldom happens. Albert Einstein took at least 10 years, between the ages of 16 and 26, to develop his theory of relativity. Most creativity involves the development and execution of original insights. Pablo Picasso constantly changed and transformed his mural masterpiece *Guernica* as he painted it. Professor Robert Weisberg, who has written extensively about this, defines creativity as *incremental* in nature, and that is an excellent way to think of it. One of the incidental benefits of the copy/art team system is that both individuals challenge and incrementally improve each other's concepts.

These factors are crucial to any consideration of advertising creativity. When they receive the advertising strategy, the creative people will start to think about – to cogitate about – how to communicate the campaign message, in a way that will arrest and interest the target market. They will be searching for a relevant idea that is innovative and impactful, one that has never been used before in advertising. It is usually easy to find innovative and original ideas that are *not* relevant, but those ideas are.... well, irrelevant. A relevant idea may or may not arrive quite quickly. But then it will need to be developed, incrementally, in all its aspects. Almost always, the initial idea will need to be chiselled, moulded, honed – particularly for use in different media. This takes time. But creative people in advertising know that time is not infinitely available. There is a commercial imperative, a deadline to be met. If a new campaign is needed by next Thursday, the creative team will need to have a new campaign ready by next Thursday. This can be exceedingly stressful. Few people realize the mental agonies advertising creative people undergo as the days pass, and the new campaign does not materialize. Every day that passes means there is one less day still available. But 9 times out of 10 – maybe 99 times out of 100 – they eventually make the deadline. If they fail too often, they will find themselves no longer working as advertising creative people.

The nature of creative people

Advertising creative people are notoriously egotistic, volatile, and irascible. If you happen to find yourself in any bar or pub frequented by advertising people in London, New York, or any of the world's other advertising capitals, you can safely bet that you will soon hear stories of punch-ups, of chairs being hurled across rooms, of computer keyboards being thrown out of windows when creative people fight about their advertising ideas. Almost all these stories are mythical, but they reflect advertising people's own image – in its way glamorous – of advertising creative people.

Likewise, if you start any broad discussion about the nature and behaviour of creative people in society, you can safely bet that within a few minutes somebody will mention Vincent Van Gogh or Paul Gauguin, or both. Why? Not because they are typical; they were not at all typical. No other artists have ended up with amputated ears, few have fled from civilization to live among native peoples on the far side of the world. But once again, Van Gogh and Gauguin epitomize our romantic image of artists: headstrong egotists, often mentally unbalanced. The reality is entirely different. The vast majority of artists – and of advertising creative people – lead exceptionally hardworking, relatively conventional lives.

Nonetheless, it is true that highly creative people are different from the rest of us in certain specific ways. Over recent years, a good deal of research has been carried out into these differences by psychologists, and more recently by neuroscientists. Their findings show that creative people do tend to be more introspective, more self-sufficient, experimental, and non-conformist. However, in no study have the differences between creative people and others been vast. If you draw a spectrum, with conformity at one end and non-conformity at the other, creative people, on average, will veer towards non-conformity. Only a few, like Van Gogh and Gauguin (and Einstein, who was decidedly eccentric), will be far out on the extreme edge. As Professor Michael Badawy, at the Virginia Polytechnic Institute, put it:

> Creativity is like height, weight and strength. People vary considerably in these dimensions, but everybody has some height, some weight and some strength. Likewise, there is a certain amount of creativity in all of us, but some of us are obviously a lot more creative than others.

There is yet another vital way in which creative people differ from others. Creative people are obsessive about their output. They wish, and expect, to be judged by their output rather than by their personal behaviour. This was well expressed by the psychologist Dr Anthony Storr:

> The work, rather than the person, becomes the focus of self-esteem. To care more about one's book or one's painting than one does about oneself will seem strange to those who are sure enough of themselves to be themselves in social relations. But if a book or a painting contains more of the real person than is ever shown in ordinary life, it is not surprising that the producer is hyper-sensitive.

How do all these factors impinge on creative people in advertising? Well, they know they are, and feel they are, different from others. They work under often intense psychological pressure. And they care obsessively about their output, which means they usually take criticism badly. Taken together, these factors do tend to make them egotistical, volatile, and quick to anger. Such behaviours may not be justifiable, but they are understandable – and must be understood by those who want to work with them, successfully.

Managing creative people

Until the 1970s, creative people in agencies were 'managed' by the agencies' top executives, through their own department head, the creative director. Creative directors were sometimes very powerful, but they seldom, if ever, ran the shop. This was the province of the businessmen who owned and built the agency. Such businessmen might be sympathetic to creativity, as was John Pearce, the guiding light at CDP. Or they might, more commonly, see creative people as a necessary evil: creative people were essential, but had far too high an opinion of their own contribution, and this fuelled their intolerable egotism and volatility. This view is reflected in the quotation from John Hobson in Chapter 1. (Research studies among advertising creative people confirm that most of them believe it is their output, the advertisements, which the rest of agency live off, and that top managements have little appreciation of this basic fact. An old advertising quip runs 'Creative people in agencies are always covered in love bites. Self-inflicted, of course.')

Hence there was continuous strife between agency managements and their creative departments. Shortly after I started working in advertising, the chairman of one of Britain's most successful agencies publicly declared that it was his ambition 'To break the stranglehold of the creative people on the production of advertising'. But with the growth of television advertising, and the creative revolution led in America by DDB and in London by CDP, much of the power in agencies moved from the business managers to the top creative people. At the very minimum, they reached parity. And in the 1960s and 1970s, many agencies, particularly in the USA, were founded by, or around, top creative people. This was a new phenomenon.

It became apparent that the division between agency managements and the newly enfranchised creative departments had to be bridged, and this was part of the genesis of *account planning* (page 14). The ingenuity of account planning was that the new account planners had twin (or even triple) loyalties. They worked closely with, and often represented, the creative people; they worked closely with, and often represented, the account handlers; (and they worked closely with, and often represented, within the agency, the clients). They were able to handle this apparent conflict of loyalties because, above all, they worked closely with and *always* represented the opinions and wishes of consumers, of the target market. As market research developed, from the 1970s onwards, the voice of the consumer was increasingly heard in advertising. In agencies, the account planners were at the epicentre of this development. They carried out, either themselves or through specialist research companies, all the testing of new creative concepts. This gave them enormous influence. Nobody in advertising can ever totally ignore the opinions of the consumer, of the target market. Consumer research into advertisements, to return to John Hobson's quotation, had been carried out previously. But this had been done in a confrontational way. The agency managers checked out the creative people's ideas, then returned to the creative people with the research findings and told them what to do. Account planning does not work like that: the creative people are integrated into the process. This was a major step forward.

It must not be thought, however, that every shred of friction between creative people and agency managements was thus eliminated at one fell swoop. Not all account planners are brilliant diplomats; not all creative people can accept criticism, even when it is put to them diplomatically. Recent studies among creative people, around the world, show that many remain suspicious of the influence of research on their creativity. They fear that the public rejects truly innovative concepts – the story of the Impressionists again – and that it is essential to take market research among the public with several large pinches of salt. This is true. But all the best creative people acknowledge that account planning can help them improve their output – incrementally, at the very least.

Account management

Had this book been written before creative and media agencies broke apart, and before account planning took hold, the opening section of this chapter would doubtless have been devoted to account managers: the people who are responsible for the liaison between clients and agencies.

Different agencies have different names for those who handle contact with their clients on a day-to-day basis: account managers, account executives, account supervisors, and others. Above these in the agency hierarchy are account directors, client service directors, or simply board directors. And in America the title president or vice-president is often used. Whatever the nomenclature, the job specifications remain the same. Account managers represent the agency to the client, and the client to the agency. At a less senior level, they handle and progress the day-to-day work the agency carries out for its clients. At a senior level, their role is more strategic, and the account director ensures the client is content (hopefully more than content) with the service the agency is providing, and that the agency's plans and campaigns are all going in the right strategic direction.

Moreover, in earlier times, the diverse variety of work carried out by agencies meant the account manager worked with the client on a multiplicity of marketing services, and was expected to oversee all of them. This meant the account manager worked closely with many of the client's marketing personnel and got to know them and their business exceedingly well, in every aspect. Nobody else in the agency knew a fraction as much about the client's business as the appointed account manager. So good account managers were very powerful. They were the lynchpins of the agency organization. They could, and frequently did, take their clients with them when they switched jobs.

Today things are not quite the same. Yes, account managers are still highly important. They are still responsible for supervising and coordinating all the work the agency does for their clients. But the work the agency does is relatively specific. The agency creates new campaigns, carries out the account planning relevant to those campaigns, and liaises with the client's media agency. Account managers orchestrate these activities. But account planners, too, develop close relationships with clients. So do creative people. So account managers have far less personal control than they did. Moreover, clients work with a raft of different marketing services companies, and their personal relationships with each of them tend to be less close than they were with the multifaceted full-service agencies of the past. Strong account mangers do still, occasionally, take their clients with them when they switch jobs, but in large agencies this happens rarely. Because in addition to all the factors listed above, most major clients are now handled internationally.

International advertising

Naturally, advertising has not been immune to the globalization of world trade. Far from it. Most global companies are also global advertisers. International cosmetics, perfume, and fashion companies have been running global campaigns – mostly in top-class fashion magazines – since the 1930s. But the rush into global advertising by mass consumer goods companies did not really get going until the end of the 20th century. And even now, the reality is that there are very few campaigns that are literally global. Most are multinational – that is, they run in many countries, but in many others, local laws, local customs, and local competitors force variations from global uniformity.

In a shrinking world, the commercial benefits of global – or anyway multinational – advertising are indisputable. Central control of campaigns is easier. International travellers see the same campaign everywhere, instead of a mish-mash of different campaigns in different countries. As national cultures become more homogeneous, campaigns that succeed in one country usually succeed in others. The transference of such knowledge from country to country is one of multinational companies' key commercial strengths. And globalization means creative costs can be amortized – though the savings from amortization are generally far less than novitiate global advertisers expect.

But while the benefits are clear, the mechanics are complicated. The world is not nearly as homogeneous as the protagonists of globalization like to claim. Almost everything changes as you move from country to country: landscape, architecture, language, laws, traditions, people's physiognomy and clothes, and often the product formulation and its packaging. Advertisements can be, and are, made to skirt around these differences, but many end up fairly bland in consequence. Hence the creation of truly effective multinational campaigns demands a great deal of inter-country discussion and coordination.

Whether or not their campaigns are homogeneous throughout the world, global advertisers usually seek to use the same creative agency throughout the world. Even if the advertisements must vary by country, for the client there is a great benefit in having a single agency that can coordinate its advertising everywhere. Consequently, all the largest agencies have structured themselves to handle international clients. They appoint global client service directors (whatever their exact title), who are responsible for the way the agency services the clients across the world. Global client service directors live in aeroplanes (and in luxury hotels), and wield considerable power – similar to the power of the account manager in the old, full-service agency. Nobody else in an agency knows nearly as much about a client and its international operations as the global client service director. And the worldwide turnover and profit of a single global client may far exceed the turnover and profit of the entire local agency in some, smaller countries.

To handle their global clients, agencies have therefore developed matrix management to a high level of sophistication. Both local and international managers have interwoven and overlapping responsibilities for services and profitability. It is a complex new game, calling for close teamwork. But agencies are rapidly learning to get good at it: they have to.

Specialist agencies

Most of this chapter has concerned general, rather than specialist, creative agencies. This is because the larger creative agencies, both nationally and internationally, are all generalists. That is, they handle the advertising needs of clients in almost every manufacturing and service sector. They willingly do so because, first, clients seldom allow their agency to handle the advertising of their competitors. An agency can work for, say, only one automobile client, one petfood client, one toiletries client, and so on. So if an agency wants to build up its business, it cannot afford to specialize in a single market sector. Second, most agency people enjoy working for clients in different sectors. They find it stimulating, and they transfer the knowledge they acquire from one sector to another. (This is one of the key reasons why advertisers are generally unable to create their own in-house agencies – though many have tried.)

However, there are a small number of specialist agencies that handle certain classes of business. Specialist agencies handle cinema advertising, theatre advertising, recruitment advertising, direct response coupon advertising (off-the-page), pharmaceutical company advertising, and technical financial advertising. In these areas, clients are seldom concerned about their agency handling competitors' campaigns. They are more concerned that the agency should be conversant with their particular commercial needs, and with any legal requirements that apply specifically to their sector – and generalist agencies seldom are.

Additionally, as noted on page 29, in recent years a group of creative agencies has emerged which specialize in Internet and other digital advertising. These agencies are usually subject to the same constraints regarding the handling of directly competitive clients as general agencies are – but clients interpret the constraints more leniently, as the digital agency sector is still relatively small, and the skills involved are relatively scarce. It is widely agreed that the creative skills involved in developing a digital campaign are different from, but similar to, the creative skills employed in other media. An article in the authoritative *International Journal of Advertising* in 2009 listed 'The Six Principles of Digital Advertising' as:

1) Advertisers must be sensitive to consumer concerns about privacy and spam.
2) Consumers are more likely to be receptive to digital ads from advertisers they trust.
3) Consumers are more likely to respond to digital ads for products that are relevant to them.
4) Digital approaches that incorporate interactivity are more likely to be effective.
5) In the digital context advertising messages that are entertaining have a higher chance of success.
6) In the long run, digital messages need to build the brand to be effective.

Several of these principles apply across all media (principles 2, 3, and 6 – and to some extent 5). The others are clearly specific to digital advertising. It is this overlap which has made it unclear whether, in the long term, digital agencies will be merged into general agencies or will continue to plough their own furrow. On this question, the jury is still out.

The creative agencies have now created the advertisements. Let us go on to explore how the media agencies will buy the space and time in which the advertisements will appear.

Chapter 6

The media agencies: spending the clients' money

In neither Britain nor the USA was the bisection and compartmentalization of creative and media-buying services universally welcomed by everyone working in advertising; nor was it entirely logical. While the split was in progress, many argued – some still argue – that selecting the media and creating the advertisements are intrinsically part of the same process: the process of producing a cost-effective advertising campaign. They complained that the split would result in each type of agency focusing myopically on their own narrow specialism and failing to see the bigger campaign picture. Though advertisers, and agency managements, have worked hard to minimize this myopia, there is some justice in the complaint. Creative and media agencies seldom communicate as thoroughly as they should, and seldom fully appreciate each other's point of view. As things currently stand, however, the trend to specialization which caused the split seems irreversible. The separation of creative and media agencies seems here to stay.

It is undeniably true that the personalities and talents of the individuals who work in each type of agency are so different as to be almost antipathetic, and it was this antipathy which, in part, led to the rift. Yes, both are called upon to think innovatively. But people in media agencies tend to be far less volatile, egotistic, and intuitive, far more grounded, numerical, and process-driven.

Though they do not need to be masters of differential calculus, and few are, the successful individuals in media agencies have an instinctive feel for figures – and they need it, because they spend a great deal of each day poring over and analysing computer data. Poring over and analysing computer data is anathema to most creative people.

Fish where the fish are – at the lowest possible cost

The simplest way to define the role of the media agency is to take an analogy from fishing. The media agency must help advertisers fish where the fish are – at the lowest possible cost. 'Fish where the fish are' is a maxim which applies to all areas of marketing, not merely advertising. The 'fish', in the analogy, are the target market. It is common sense for fishermen to fish where the fish are; a fisherman would get nowhere fishing where no fish are to be found. Likewise, marketers will get nowhere advertising in media where none of the target market will see the advertisements.

But the analogy goes deeper. Before deciding where they are going to fish, fishermen must take into account the cost. It will generally cost an angler more to go where there is an abundance of fish to be caught, especially if the fish are of a particularly high quality; similarly, a trawler captain will carefully assess the cost of sailing any distance to find a large shoal of fish, in order to ensure the trawl is profitable.

Finding the best place to find the fish – which equals identifying the best media in which to find the target market – is the first, strategic role of the media agency. Ensuring that the fishing is then as cheap as possible is the second role of the media agency.

In a media agency, these two roles are called *planning* and *buying*. The former is the strategic role, the latter calls for great negotiating skill. Although media rates and prices are published, the costs of buying campaigns are highly negotiable. But the two roles are not quite as separate as they may sound: planning and buying must be welded together. A negotiated price will only be a bargain if it meets the strategy of the campaign. Buying cheap space simply because it is cheap is patently a waste of money. (It is the equivalent of paying nothing to fish in a place where there are no fish!) So not all media agencies separate the two roles. Some media agencies employ individuals called 'planner/buyers' who do both jobs, others divide planners from buyers, though the two individuals must work closely together. Naturally, the different agencies which follow the two different structural routes are all convinced their route is the best one.

Whatever its internal structure, the strategic first role of the media agency will be to select and recommend which broad media sector or sectors should be used to reach the target market: newspapers, magazines, television, radio, direct mail, posters and transport, cinema – or the Internet. Or a combination of several of these. The media agency will reach this decision in collaboration with the advertiser, and usually with the creative agency too. The advertising strategy document will, as always, play a key role. The advertising strategy will have defined the key objectives of the campaign. The broad media selection will then seek to meet these objectives, and as we shall see, it will be based on three fundamental factors: the budget available, the technical nature of the medium, and the medium's coverage of the target market.

Once the medium, or the combination of media, has been chosen, the media agency will refine its recommendations further. It will select and recommend the precise details of how, where, and when the campaign should appear, within the chosen media. These decisions will again be discussed with the advertiser, and possibly with the creative agency, but this is the primary territory of the media agency. Planning and implementing the detailed placing of the campaign are the media agency's key expertise.

Selecting the medium

As stated above, the three fundamental factors involved in selecting which media sector to use for a campaign – the budget, the nature of the medium, and the coverage of the target market – interact. All three must be taken into account when a campaign is being planned. There are no prizes for getting two right if the third is wrong: you will not achieve two-thirds of the hoped-for results – you will be lucky to get any results at all.

The budget

Manifestly, the size of the available budget will be a prime factor in choosing which medium to use. However, nowadays all media sectors are highly diverse, which means they are highly flexible. For any given campaign, it is possible to buy large advertisements or small ones, to buy many advertisements or few, to buy advertisements that will reach large numbers of people or small numbers of people. In every case, the price of the advertisements, and thus of the total campaign, will vary. As in most purchasing situations, bigger buyers get quantity discounts, even if the exact nature of such discounts may not always be readily apparent. (For example, the cost per second for a 30-second spot is cheaper than the cost per second for a 15-second spot, as television companies prefer to sell longer spots – but a novice buyer may not notice this.)

So there is no fixed entry price for any one medium. Today there are so many media, and so many advertisers, that media prices reflect supply and demand very precisely: in economic terms, the market for advertising is a free market, open and highly competitive. By buying selectively, and knowledgeably, an advertiser can make a small budget go a long way – with the aid, that is, of a topnotch media agency. Nonetheless, it is unwise to try and stretch a small budget too far. The available budget might be sufficient to buy, say, one whole page in a mass-circulation national newspaper. But if so, that would seldom be the best way to spend the money. In normal circumstances, for most campaigns, more and smaller advertisements in that same newspaper, or more large advertisements in newspapers with smaller circulations, would both be better options. (But if the advertising strategy called for maximum impact on a single day, the whole page in the mass-circulation newspaper *might* be the right thing to do.)

Television is a good example of how all this works. Overall, national television is the most expensive medium. But there are now many specialist television stations with relatively small audiences, where advertising spots are relatively cheap. You pay for what you get: the smaller the audience, the lower the price. Likewise, spots can be bought quite cheaply on even the largest television stations when audiences are small: in the middle of the night, say. Once again, the smaller the audience, the lower the price. Consequently, many advertisers with fairly small budgets exploit the lower prices available from the cheaper television stations, and the cheaper times – while advertisers selling mass consumer goods need to reach mass audiences, and so there is little point in them buying spots that are seen by only a few people. These same principles apply, suitably adapted, across all media.

The nature of the medium

For advertising, every media sector has, by its very nature, certain inherent characteristics. Most of these are plain common sense. Television, cinema, and the Internet have sound, vision, and movement. Radio has only sound. Newspapers and magazines provide space for long copy, which people can read at their leisure, and they are highly portable. Posters have the impact of size, and can be sited near retailers where customers make their purchases. Direct mail and emails can be highly personalized.

Despite the welter of market research that is nowadays available, none of these characteristics can be exactly quantified in financial terms. However, the varying characteristics provide varying advantages for different kinds of product. The skill, for the advertiser and their media and creative agencies, lies in selecting the medium which is most appropriate – that is, likely to be most persuasive – for the product or service being advertised. Some products demand the kind of explanation that only printed copy can provide; some products need to emphasize their appetite appeal, using high-quality colour photography or cinematography; some products can be perfectly well advertised using sound alone; some products benefit from the personal feel of a letter. Using the nature of a medium to its full advantage will maximize the effectiveness of a campaign – and often make a limited budget punch well above its weight. It is always 'horses for courses'.

Coverage of the target market

Without further belabouring the 'fish where the fish are' analogy, this is the absolutely key factor in choosing the right medium. If the medium does not reach the people who may make a purchase, the advertising is totally wasted. It might be thought that the 'safe' way to avoid such a danger is to advertise in media which reach, as near as possible, 100% of the national population: if *everybody* in the country sees the campaign, then the target market will, by definition, have been reached. Very nearly 100% of the population *can* be reached by television, by a blanket national press or poster campaign, or by a blanket national direct mail campaign of the kind the government employs when wishing to communicate with the entire country. However, this 'safe' route ignores the second part of the 'fish' analogy. Taking this route will almost invariably be unnecessarily expensive. It is therefore unlikely to be the most cost-effective route possible. In reaching 100% or thereabouts, the advertiser will inevitably be paying for advertising that will reach a huge number of people who will *not* make a purchase. In other words, the campaign will waste a fair proportion of the available budget.

To spend the budget as cost-effectively as possible, and thus reach the fish at the lowest possible cost, the target market will need to be defined with considerable accuracy, and this group will then need to be correlated with its media usage. Market research surveys such as the Target Group Index will be an invaluable tool in correlating the coverage of the target market achieved by different media sectors. And often the advertiser will then decide that the cost of reaching close to 100% of the target market is too high – that it is more cost-effective to achieve a lower coverage, more cheaply. (To go for fewer fish, at far less expense.) The media agency will be able to provide the advertiser with a chart showing the incremental costs of reaching, for example, 60% / 70% / 80% / 90%...of the target market. The advertiser will then be able to make an informed judgement regarding the level of coverage to be aimed for, at an acceptable cost.

Having selected the basic media sector, or sectors, the media agency will get down to planning the detail of the campaign.

Size, frequency, and timing

To a large extent, the principal expertise of a media agency is to choose between trade-offs. Once the size of the budget has been set, and the selection of the media sector(s) to be used has been determined, the media agency must slice up the available money in the most cost-effective way between the key media.

If the advertiser's budget were infinite, unlimited, then the media agency would be able to achieve 100% coverage of the target market, with huge advertisements and lengthy commercials, which would appear constantly, without cease. But no budget, of any kind, is ever infinite or unlimited. This unrealistic picture of a fairy-tale campaign highlights the need for the trade-offs. The media agency has to recommend, as we have seen, what percentage of the target market it is economical to reach – and then how big the advertisements should be, how often they should appear, and how long the campaign should run.

Again, all these factors interact. If bigger advertisements or longer commercials are used, this will mean they must appear less frequently. Similarly, if it is necessary for the campaign to run for an extended period of time, it will be necessary for the advertisements to be smaller (or shorter), or to appear less frequently – or possibly both. When a campaign is being planned, there are no precise right and wrong answers to most of these questions. But a good media agency, employing a combination of numerical analysis and past experience, will be able to offer the advertiser clear guidelines. The question of the advertisement's size (or duration) will need to be discussed and agreed with both the creative agency and the advertiser; the frequency and duration of the campaign will mainly be discussed and agreed with the advertiser – though the creative agency will be kept 'in the loop'.

The size of the advertisement will be determined by the extent to which the *awareness* and *impact* are key objectives within the advertising strategy. This is truer of printed and outdoor media than of broadcast media. The public naturally spots the size of a printed advertisement, or a poster, but is much less acutely aware of the length of a television or radio commercial. Generally, the larger a print advertisement, the greater the number of people who will notice it. And at a subconscious level, the public realizes that a larger advertisement is probably about something 'important'. So larger advertisements achieve high awareness and high impact.

But sometimes, surprisingly, these factors are relatively unimportant. Perhaps the product is only used by a small number of people, a small target market. In certain circumstances – remembering there are advertisements which look for people, and advertisements which people look for – smaller advertisements can be far more cost-effective than larger ones. If you are advertising a cough medicine, for example, you only really want the advertisement to be seen by people suffering from a cough. So a small advertisement with the headline 'Bad Cough?' will flag down people suffering – and they are the precise target market.

Similar criteria apply with regard to timing and frequency. Most people plan their summer holidays in the depths of winter – so holiday companies advertise heavily around Christmas and the New Year. Most new cars are bought in the spring and early summer, so automobile advertisers focus on those months. Fashions change in the spring and autumn, so that is when new styles will be advertised, while of course coughs and colds are more likely in the winter, so that is when their medicine campaigns appear. Many of the products people buy are seasonal – but many are not. In these cases, advertisers may aim to boost sales by running campaigns when their competitors are not doing so. Or they may go for short, sharp campaigns of high frequency to dominate the market for a specific period. (Procter and Gamble, the world's largest advertiser, is a great believer in short, sharp, intense bursts of advertising.) In making all these decisions, the media agency will be greatly influenced by past experience. They will know about campaigns that have been run in past years, and how long they have lasted. Like military strategists, they will aim constantly to surprise their clients' competitors by out-manoeuvring them.

Just as the creative agency will constantly be looking for innovative and impactful ways to communicate the advertising messages, the media agency will constantly be looking for innovative and impactful ways to spend the available budget – so long as it reaches the right fish, at the lowest possible cost.

Internet and digital

As was emphasized in Chapter 2, digital advertising has been enjoying rapid growth throughout the world. So far, this growth has almost entirely involved the Internet, rather than telephony. As with creative agencies, media agencies have split into generalists – agencies that handle the entire range of available advertising media; and digital specialists, which focus exclusively on digital media. At the moment, the greater part of Internet advertising is handled by the generalist agencies, but, as in the creative sphere, this situation is fluid and could easily change over the coming years.

Whether generalist or specialist, media agencies have to be conversant with the quite different types of advertising that appear on the Internet, of which the three most important are:

- *Display advertising* – banners, pop-ups, sponsorships, and other 'intrusive' communications which work in much the same way and with the same objectives as all display advertising. They aim to bring the brand to the attention of the target market by building awareness – and sometimes, but not always, they offer the opportunity to click through from the advertisement to the advertiser's website. Display advertising accounts for around 20% of all Internet advertising revenue.

- *Search advertising* – 'search' is the great strength of the Internet, and accounts for approximately 60% of all Internet advertising revenue (the remaining percentage of Internet advertising is accounted for by recruitment classifieds). It is most similar to, in traditional advertising, directory and classified advertising. But its speed and comprehensiveness are unique to the Internet. Search companies – such as Google, Yahoo!, and MSN – carry advertisers' announcements in listings which encourage people to click-through to the advertiser's website to find out more, and often to buy what they want, directly, online. The position of the advertiser's listing on the screen will hugely influence the response it achieves. Research has shown that the first announcements seen by anyone searching, or surfing, the Internet gather the greatest number of click-throughs. Advertisers therefore pay the search companies a premium to be at the top, or near the top, of their listings.

- *Websites* – websites are most similar, in terms of traditional media, to leaflets, brochures, and catalogues. As with 'search', the user takes the initiative and seeks out the website, either via a search listing or directly via its domain name. The situation is complicated by the fact that not all websites are commercial. Many individuals, and many groups, design and build their own websites. There is no charge for this, beyond the cost of building and registering the site. The 'cost' of websites is therefore not included in Internet advertising expenditure data. Major advertisers, especially retailers, sell directly from their websites, making websites an exceptionally cost-efficient way to obtain sales.

As the Internet continues to develop, new means of advertising – via blogs and social networking sites, for example – continuously come on stream, though most of them find it hard to capture as much advertising revenue as they hoped for.

Like television, the Internet is highly effective for targeting different demographic groups, by special interests, activities, and at different times during the day and night. Internet users can be identified, and their purchasing and other characteristics can be related directly to them. This makes personal Internet targeting far more accurate than any other.

Display advertising on the Internet is charged and paid for in much the same way as display advertising in other media. The rate paid by the advertiser is determined by the size and nature of the audience reached, and by the size and nature of the advertisement itself. And as has already been noted, there is no 'media charge' for posting a website.

'Search' advertising, however, has developed its own unique means of charging: *pay per click*. How much the advertiser pays the search company for appearing on its site will depend on precisely how many times Internet users click-through from the listing to the advertiser's website. This means that the advertiser's cost will be directly related to the number of visitors the website receives, and almost certainly will then be related, albeit less directly, to sales achieved. This close relationship makes the evaluation of Internet search advertising more quantifiable than most other forms of advertising – though no more quantifiable than traditional direct mail.

The campaign is now ready to 'go to bed'. The creative work has been completed by the creative agency, the media have been chosen and bought by the media agency. The advertiser has approved the entire package, and the starting gun is at the ready. Throughout the development process, market research will have been used – and it will continue to be used to check the progress of the campaign once it is launched. Let us now look at how market research fits into the picture.

Chapter 7
Research, research, research

Early days

Advertising can be so expensive, so complex, and the results so unpredictable, that advertisers have long sought to formulate rules which, like scientific laws, will guarantee results. They have hoped there might be a Golden Key, as mentioned at the start of this book, which would unlock the secret of sales success. In physics, scientists know that if they do A, then B will follow; if they do Y, then Z will follow. Might there be some way of achieving the same in advertising? Over 100 years ago there was already a seat of Advertising Psychology at North-Western University, Chicago. The Professor of Advertising Psychology, Professor Walter Dill Scott, addressed the advertising industry Agate Club in 1901 on the subject: 'The Psychology of Involuntary Attention as Applied to Advertising', and in 1909 he published a book titled *The Psychology of Advertising*. This was the first of countless studies that have aimed to show, in psychological terms, exactly how advertising works.

Some 14 years later, in 1923, still searching for the elusive Golden Key, one of the greatest American advertising copywriters of all time, Claude Hopkins, published a book called *Scientific Advertising*. To today's generation of advertising people, the notion that anyone could have claimed to turn advertising into a science nearly a century ago is more than a trifle ludicrous. Nonetheless, Hopkins's book became – and still is – a classic. Hopkins specialized in direct response, coupon advertising, where the results of advertisements can be exactly measured by counting the coupons sent in. Using the coupon response data he acquired over many decades, he developed rules for writing successful advertisements, and many of his rules remain true today – for coupon advertisements. But they do not necessarily hold true for uncouponed advertisements for branded goods; and of course, radio, television, and many other modern advertising media did not even exist in 1923. However, the attempt to turn advertising into a science did not cease. But as worldwide advertising expenditures fell during the 1930s Great Depression, and during and after the Second World War, there was a lull in activity.

By the early 1950s, advertising had started to boom again. In the USA, a new movement that believed it had found the Golden Key emerged in New York and Chicago. This was called *motivation research*, sometimes called *depth research*, and it was loosely based on Freudian psychoanalytic theory. Its thesis was that consumers' buying behaviour was more often emotional than rational, and was influenced – indeed controlled – by people's subconscious desires. The research technique employed trained psychologists or psychotherapists to carry out lengthy, one-to-one interviews with consumers, probing their subconscious minds in much the same way as would be done in clinical analysis. These one-to-ones were, and still are, called 'depth interviews'. Two highly competitive men each claimed to be the 'father' of this type of research: Dr Ernest Dichter (much the more famous) and Louis Cheskin. Both had trained as psychologists and had psychoanalytic experience, and both claimed to have started experimenting with the use of depth probings in the 1930s, even though they did not come to the fore until two decades later.

Motivation research is the subject of what is still the best-known and best-selling book about advertising ever written: *The Hidden*

Persuaders, by Vance Packard (1957). In this book, Dichter, Cheskin, and others make impressive claims regarding the powers of their research techniques. Dr Dichter, for example, claims that successful advertising:

> manipulates human motivations and desires and develops a need for goods with which the public has at one time been unfamiliar – perhaps even undesirous of purchasing.

He also claims: 'We undress people in terms of their rationalisations.'

Such claims caused great concern to many members of the public, who did not like the idea of their rationalizations being 'undressed', nor their motivations and desires being psychologically manipulated. It made them sound like puppets on advertising strings. And this was the scary theme of Vance Packard's book, which made it such a sales success. This was the era when 'brainwashing' was much talked about, largely as a consequence of the show trials in the communist USSR, where those accused were 'brainwashed' into parroting their confessions robotically. Or so it was believed. The American Central Intelligence Agency (CIA) was neurotically obsessed about the putative ability of communist regimes to exert mind control. (The classic brainwashing movie, *The Manchurian Candidate*, was made in 1962.) But the power to control people's brains, in the ways many then feared, has never existed – and it has certainly never existed in advertising. It must never be forgotten that the claims of researchers – and indeed of advertising people themselves – are often boastful and self-serving. It is in their financial interests to convince advertisers that their researches, and their advertising, are exceptionally potent. This way they win more clients, and the clients spend more money on advertising. So their claims should be taken with sizable pinches of salt: they are frequently exaggerated, and sometimes downright untruthful.

This was unquestionably so in the case of what became, and remains, one of the most notorious pieces of 'research' in advertising history. In 1957, an American market researcher called James Vicary claimed to have substantially increased the sales of Coca-Cola and popcorn in a cinema in Fort Lee, New Jersey, by flashing the messages 'Drink Coca-Cola' and 'Eat Popcorn' on the cinema screen so quickly the audience did not consciously see the messages at all. He dubbed this process 'subliminal advertising' – from the Latin *sub* (beneath) and *limen* (sensory perception). Vicary's findings immediately aroused a welter of public disquiet. Vance Packard publicized the Vicary experiment in the second edition of *The Hidden Persuaders*. People everywhere grew profoundly alarmed about being manipulated by subliminal advertising without knowing it was happening. In Britain, subliminal advertising was almost immediately banned by the television authorities. But Vicary had never persuaded anyone, subliminally, to buy Coca-Cola and popcorn. In 1962, he admitted the whole thing had been a hoax, and nobody has ever been able to replicate the experiment he claimed to have carried out. Subliminal advertising, which people still talk about and agonize about, has never existed. (Recent studies have shown that subliminal communications of various kinds can occur, but there is no proof they can be used in advertising.)

Nonetheless, the phrases 'hidden persuaders' and 'subliminal advertising' entered the vernacular, and became common usage. So much so that the title of the next highly questionable investigation into the powers of advertising was *Subliminal Seduction*, a book published in 1975 by Professor Wilson Bryan Key of the University of Western Ontario. *Subliminal Seduction*, like *The Hidden Persuaders* before it, became a best-seller by playing on the public's fear of being manipulated by 'secret' advertising messages – though it was not nearly as successful as its predecessor.

Professor Key believed that messages promising sexual success were encrypted – he used the word 'embedded' – in

14. James Vicary: his 1957 experiment with 'subliminal advertising' in New Jersey was a hoax

advertisements. He claimed that these embeddings, like subliminal advertising (which had already been disproved), were not seen consciously but nonetheless controlled consumers' behaviour. Professor Key claimed:

> Every major advertising agency has at least one embedding technician in its art department. The technique is taught at most commercial art schools.

This is codswallop. There is not, and never has been, any such thing as an 'embedding technician' in an advertising agency. But once again, the belief that all, or most, advertising works by promising sexual success has stuck. Countless media articles and debates are built on the belief that sex constantly perks up advertising, and that sex will sell anything: sex is the long-searched-for Golden Key. This is codswallop too. There is almost no sex in advertising, though most people refuse to believe it. There are sexy advertisements for perfumes and cosmetics, for fashion and lingerie – all products where a little eroticism hardly comes amiss. Mildly sexy advertisements for other products come and go, but when an ice cream (Haagen-Dazs) had the temerity to use playful but innocuous sexy images in its British campaign, the attendant flurry of nudge-nudge, wink-wink publicity beggared belief. This would never have happened if raunchy advertising were commonplace. It would be astonishing if sex were completely absent from advertisements. But are there sexy advertisements for supermarkets, for household cleansers, for medicines, for financial products? Hardly ever.

The public insist they do not like sex dragged into campaigns irrelevantly, and about one-fifth of the complaints to the UK Advertising Standards Authority concern taste and decency. Moreover, nowadays more than 40% of consumer spending is by the over-50s. They aren't all celibate, but lust is perhaps not uppermost in their minds. For all these reasons, advertisements veer towards the prim rather than the prurient. You will never see remotely explicit sex, or full-frontal nudity, in advertisements in the UK or USA. Compared to the media that surround them, advertisements portray a veritably sanitized world – unrealistic in being far too prudish, rather than too licentious.

The unique selling proposition

Almost all of the above theories came from people outside of advertising: academics and researchers. But one of the most celebrated and influential advertising research processes came from within an advertising agency – and it helped build that agency into one of the largest in the world. The agency in question was called after its founder, Ted Bates. The Ted Bates agency was convinced it had found the elusive Golden Key. Starting in New York, Ted Bates's agency quickly built itself into a worldwide network. The advertising process it developed is always known by its public 'face', the *unique selling proposition* (USP). But in reality, the USP process is a complete campaign development system, in which research plays an integral part.

The USP system certainly starts out by stating that all advertising campaigns should search for, and single-mindedly hammer home, the single fact about a brand which differentiates it from its competitors and will make people buy: the USP. But once this USP has been identified, and incorporated into a campaign, the research aspects of the system kick in. When the campaign is running, the public's awareness of the USP is tracked by research – a measurement we'll return to in the next section – and two figures are calculated:

1) The percentage of the public who buy the brand and who know the advertising USP.
2) The percentage of the public who buy the brand but do not know the advertising USP.

The difference between (1) and (2) Ted Bates called '*usage pull*'. As long as (1) is larger than (2) – the agency claimed – the extent by which it was larger represented the additional percentage of the population the USP had persuaded to buy the brand. This sounds logical: if more people who know the USP buy the brand, presumably it is the USP that has persuaded them to buy. And the greater the difference between (1) and (2), the greater the power of the USP. If (2) was more or less the same as (1), then the USP was not persuading anybody extra to buy the brand: the USP was unpersuasive. And in those unusual cases where (2) was larger than (1) – where among those who knew the USP, fewer people bought the brand than those who did not know it – the USP was actually putting people off, the usage pull was negative. A campaign that did not demonstrate sufficiently positive usage pull would itself be pulled off air.

Ted Bates claimed that by accurately identifying USPs, and then measuring their usage pull, they could significantly increase advertising effectiveness. And from the early 1940s until the late 1960s, the Bates agency developed and publicized this system with immense success. During those years, the agency did indeed produce some highly effective campaigns for their clients – particularly for the Mars Corporation, for many years their largest international client – and this in turn persuaded many more clients to appoint them. The USP was Bates's own USP, and its usage pull among clients was considerable.

However, over the decades, three changes occurred that seriously undermined the USP system. First, researchers showed that people who regularly use a brand – any brand – are far more likely to know its advertising than people who do not use it. This is called 'feedback'. So usage pull was back-to-front. It isn't knowing the advertising that persuades you to use a brand: if you use a brand, you tend to know its advertising. Or to be still more exact, both things happen at once, and causation either way is impossible to prove.

Second, as economies grew more affluent, and more and more products came onto the market, the functional differences between different brands often became imperceptible. The main differences were brand image differences – the public perceived the brands differently, sometimes knowing full well they had all but indistinguishable product specifications. So brand image advertising grew in importance, and the importance of traditional USP advertising dwindled.

Third, and associated with this, the USP system was highly verbal. A USP must be a fact expressed in words, so that people's recall of it is easy to assess. But conveying brand images may be more visual than verbal, and many commercials may also employ powerful (wordless) music. As Dr Dichter had insisted, consumers often buy products for emotional rather than rational reasons – reasons they themselves may not be able to identify, let alone put into words.

The USP system went out of fashion, and with it Ted Bates's own usage pull. However, the basic principle of identifying the single fact which differentiates a brand from its competitors, where one such fact can be identified, remains a key factor in most modern advertising strategies.

Research today

Advertising research today has naturally absorbed much of this historic learning, and has long ago stopped searching for an over-arching Golden Key. Research today deals with the separate parts of the advertising process bit by bit, seeking to improve potency and effectiveness incrementally as the campaign develops. It is unlikely that anybody now working in advertising believes there will ever be a holistic, scientific thesis which will guarantee the effectiveness of all campaigns. Everyone recognizes that advertising is far too complex, and too heterogeneous, for this to be possible.

The principal division in campaign research today is between pre-testing and post-launch tracking. Most of the former is carried out under the aegis of the creative agencies; most of the latter is carried out under the aegis of the advertisers, employing their own chosen research companies.

Pre-testing

As we have seen, a campaign starts to take shape when agency account planners have drawn up an advertising strategy, and this has been agreed by their colleagues and by their client. The strategy will include what the advertising campaign must communicate, and to which target market. In the chapter on agencies and creativity, we saw that account planners return to the campaign development process once the creative team has come up with its initial ideas, or concepts. At this stage, they test out the concepts on a sample of the target market.

This testing is almost always carried out in focus groups of eight to ten people, though one-to-one interviews, of the kind pioneered by the motivation researchers, may also occasionally be used. It is vitally important for the interviewees – whether in groups or individually – to be drawn from members of the target market. If the wrong sample is interviewed, the results will not only be irrelevant, they may positively be misleading. To give a simple example: if saloon car drivers are interviewed about a sports car advertisement, they are likely to be highly concerned about the car's safety, and to want safety information highlighted in the advertising. Sports car drivers, in contrast, will be relatively unconcerned about safety, but extremely interested in driving performance and handling. As the saloon car drivers are most unlikely to buy the sports car, incorporating their opinions will positively negate the effectiveness of the campaign. But surprising as it may seem, such mistakes are frequently made.

In a focus group, eight to ten people are brought together, and they discuss the creative concepts shown to them, under the guidance of a skilled group leader – usually an experienced market researcher or account planner. The advantages of focus groups over one-to-one interviews are threefold. Focus groups are far less expensive; they are faster – interviewing eight to ten people at once is inevitably quicker to accomplish than interviewing them individually; and above all, the group members provoke reactions from each other interactively, which the group leader will be able to encourage them to explore together. The disadvantages of focus groups are that the individuals will not have much time to express their personal views; consequently, it is almost impossible to probe deeply into individual responses; and shy individuals may get trampled upon by others – though experienced group leaders aim to ensure this does not happen. It has also been shown that even experienced group leaders tend to influence what the respondents say, try as they may to avoid doing so. (This also occurs in one-to-ones.)

Almost always, several focus groups will be carried out – relying on a single group is far too chancy – and the person who has handled them will consolidate the findings, listening again and again to tape recordings of the discussions, and studying the responses carefully. He or she will then meet the creative team, together with the account executive, and go through the findings. If certain of the findings are negative, the creative team will usually be able to amend the advertisement concept so that it overcomes the target market's concerns. But sometimes this is not possible, and the idea or ideas have to be totally abandoned. Then it is back to the drawing board! As has been said above, creative teams do not generally like their work being criticized and picked apart in this way – and they sometimes argue fiercely with the research findings – but in the end, they have to accept the system.

Only when an advertisement concept has come through this process with flying colours will it be presented, together with the findings of the research, to the client. The famous 1990s 'Guinness Surfers' commercial (loosely based on Moby Dick) which in May 2000 was voted by the British public 'The Best British Advertisement Ever' is a fine example of the account planning process in action. Account planners repeatedly researched it, and its future was often in jeopardy until creative solutions could be found to the problems the research uncovered. This all took over a year – but the outcome was worth it.

On the track

Tracking studies began in the 1950s, but did not become the dominant form of post-launch campaign evaluation until the 1990s. As their name implies, tracking studies track the impact of a campaign after it has begun, with regular surveys. The survey questions can cover many areas: respondents' recall of the advertising campaign, or of different parts of the campaign; respondents' attitudes to the campaign – what they thought was good/bad, what they found interesting/uninteresting, what they liked/disliked, what they found persuasive/unpersuasive, and so on.

The tracking surveys may be carried out monthly, bi-monthly, or quarterly. Less frequent surveys hardly 'track' a campaign, but may be employed when the campaign utilizes irregular bursts of advertising, as lightweight campaigns frequently do. It is vital for each successive tracking survey to use precisely the same questions as its predecessors, to be comparable, and each survey must interview exactly matched samples of respondents. Even the tiniest changes in question wording or in sample structure can produce wild and seemingly inexplicable fluctuations in response levels. Consistency also makes it possible to aggregate normative data. Over the years, research companies and advertisers have learned what levels of response are averagely achievable, for any given level of advertising expenditure, in any given market.

Generally speaking, the tracking data which carries most weight is advertising awareness: what percentage of the public remembers the advertising? The presupposition is that consumers will not respond to advertising they cannot remember. However, it has frequently been shown that consumers may not be influenced by advertising they do remember, while sometimes consumers are influenced by advertising they do not remember, at least not consciously. So advertising awareness is only an approximate, proxy guide to campaign effectiveness, even though it is widely used as a useful, rough and ready, assessment.

Nor is 'awareness' as straightforward as it sounds. As we saw in the section on USPs, awareness is strongly influenced by 'feedback'. Hence major brands, used by large swathes of the population, tend automatically to achieve higher awareness levels than smaller brands, used by minorities. And there are great differences between spontaneous (or top-of-mind) awareness and prompted awareness ('Do you remember any advertising for chocolate?' versus 'Do you remember this advertisement for Mars Bars?'). Verbal, factual messages are easier to remember, or anyway easier to relate during research interviews, than visual or emotive messages. Higher levels of awareness are usually generated by 'public' media – television, print, posters, for example – than by 'private' and tightly targeted media (direct mail, emails, and text messages, for example). But although tightly targeted media generate low awareness, they may be exceptionally sales-effective among those to whom they have been personally addressed.

Despite these caveats, many advertisers now set *key performance indicators* (KPIs) based on tracking results. For example: 'The KPI for the advertising at the end of the campaign is an awareness level of xx%, which must be achieved – or else!' If the campaign does not achieve the targeted KPI, it may well be pulled off air: the advertiser may feel that continuing to run it would be a waste of money. So agencies live in mortal fear that the next tracking result for a campaign they have produced will be a poor one. This is not unwarranted: agencies have been fired for consistently achieving poor tracking ratings.

Few experienced advertisers believe tracking studies are the be-all and end-all of post-launch campaign evaluation – but they have become much the most widely used system.

Other techniques

Though focus groups (pre-campaign launch) and tracking studies (post-launch) have become the standard means of advertising evaluation, researchers regularly invent new techniques which they hope will be more accurate, or more subtle, than these. Almost always, such new techniques are heavily publicized by the researchers who invent them, and garner a great deal of publicity at first – then fade away.

In the 1960s, for example, for a short while pupil dilation became a fashionable measurement technique. Psychologists had shown that respondent's pupils unconsciously dilate when they are shown images they greatly like (an attractive girl shown to young males, for example), and their pupils shrink when they are shown images they dislike (prisoners in Nazi concentration camps, for example). The eyes can be photographed while they view the images, and the pupil changes measured. It was therefore hypothesized that pupil dilation would be a good way of measuring people's responses to advertisements. However, the differences caused by advertisements are far smaller than those caused by more extreme visuals – and anyway, during the transmission of a television commercial pupil size changes constantly, especially in response to lighter and darker images. So pupil dilation failed to catch on.

Eye-tracking – following how eyes move when they look at things – has been used by psychologists in laboratories for around a century. But more recently commercial use has been made of infra-red eye-tracking goggles, which are portable and which show precisely how the eye wanders. This technique can be helpful in exploring the ways people absorb different parts of an advertisement, particularly a print advertisement. But it is no measurement of advertising persuasiveness.

Other devices that can be helpful include tachistoscopes, where an advertisement is revealed for shorter and shorter intervals and respondents are asked what they can see – rather as in an optician's eye test. Sweat measurement is an indicator of involvement and excitement. Interest dials, where respondents twist a small dial while watching commercials to show the parts of the commercial they find or do not find interesting, can reveal useful information. And most recently, brain mapping, where people's brain responses are MRI-scanned while they are shown advertisements and – it is once again hoped – the scans will reveal their true, unconscious responses. Some researchers hold out great hopes for MRI brain-scanning techniques for this purpose. All that can be said at the moment is that they are a long way off producing any really useful data.

Chapter 8
The good, the bad, and the ugly

'The all-deafening blast of puffery'

Perhaps because it is so intrusive, and perhaps because people are suspicious of its manipulative powers, advertising has long been subject to criticism, antagonism, and fear – far more so in Britain than in the USA. The snooty attitude of the British aristocracy, and of British intellectuals, to trade and commerce of all kinds is of long standing, as is their distaste for selling and salesmen. These attitudes are much less prevalent (though not totally unknown) on the other side of the Atlantic. As long ago as 1830, the British essayist and historian Thomas Macaulay, decrying advertising, wrote: 'We expect some reserve, some decent pride, in our hatter and bootmaker.' Not long afterwards, the Scottish intellectual Thomas Carlyle was similarly sour about what he called 'the all-deafening blast of puffery'. By the end of the 19th century, an influential pressure group called SCAPA (Society for Controlling Abuses of Public Advertising) published a membership list that included many of the most notable writers and artists of the day. William Morris, Rudyard Kipling, Holman Hunt, Sir Arthur Quiller-Couch, and Sir John Millais were all SCAPA members. But the public was apathetic; 500 copies of a SCAPA pamphlet were printed, only 30 were sold.

This broad pattern of response to advertising has continued ever since. Many, perhaps most, writers, academics, and even politicians are to a greater or lesser extent antagonistic to advertising, a hostility which the mass of the public does not share. However, the former group controls many of the levers of power in society. So, ever since the middle of the 19th century, advertising has been increasingly hedged about by laws and controls – probably more than any other single trade.

This was spotlit when commercial television came to Britain in 1955. While the Bill that introduced commercial television was passing through the House of Lords, Lord Reith, the intense, puritan Scot who was the driving force behind the development of the BBC from 1922 to 1938, compared the introduction of television advertising with the introduction into Britain of smallpox, the Black Death, and the bubonic plague. Other noble lords felt similarly. Lord Hailsham likened commercial television to 'a Caliban emerging from his slimy cavern'. Lord Esher forecast 'a planned and premeditated orgy of vulgarity'. Most of these horrific fears were based on what many British intellectuals believed was the coarse and crass nature of American television. The public did not share these fears; they welcomed commercial television with open arms.

However, parliament exerted its austere powers. The Act that brought British commercial television into being enshrined precepts which determinedly differentiated it from the dreaded American model. In particular, advertisements would have to be totally separated from programmes – hence the invention of the 'commercial break' – and the total quantity of advertising permitted would be strictly controlled (initially just 6 minutes per hour). A statutory committee would control standards of advertising, and this committee would draw up a set of rules which would have to be precisely followed. British viewers, the parliamentarians believed, needed to be protected from the excesses of American commercialization – and they were. Before a commercial can be made in Britain, the script has to be approved, to ensure it meets the required advertising rules. After it has been filmed, it has to be approved again, to ensure the script has been rendered accurately, with no liberties taken. The regulator's interpretation of the advertising rules is meticulous, and both advertisers and agencies have constantly railed against how unimaginatively the rules are applied. But the parliamentary Act, and its successor Acts, insist the rules be minutely adhered to.

The Advertising Standards Authority

From its inception, then, television advertising in Britain was statutorily controlled. But the situation in other media was very different. The press, in particular, had battled hard for its freedoms during the 18th and 19th centuries, when politicians had constantly tried to handcuff it and restrict what it could say. While these battles primarily concerned editorial freedoms, they also involved advertising freedoms. Advertisers were free to say what they liked, as long as they did not break the law – and it is fair to say that many less than scrupulous advertisers pushed their freedom to the limit. In the mid-19th century, advertisers would promise to cure every malady known to mankind and quite a few that were not – such as 'DEATH in the Boot, is the new affliction with which all who wear footwear are threatened' – safely cured, one is relieved to hear, by 'O'Brien's Patent Watertight Waist Foothold Golosh'. Nor were our American cousins to be outdone. In New York, a Dr Scott invented an extensive range of 'electric' products utilizing the almost magical power of the then recently discovered electricity. One was an 'Electric Cigarette'. Another was 'Dr. Scott's Electric Plaster – A NEW INVENTION – electrically cured Colds, Coughs and Chest Pains, Nervous, Muscular and Neuralgic pains, Stomach, Kidney and Liver Pains, Dyspeptic, Malarial and other Pains, Rheumatism, Gout and Inflammation', all achieved 'IN ONE TO THREE HOURS...if not entirely satisfactory the price will be cheerfully refunded'. So the evidence is unequivocal. Left to their own devices, advertisers will eagerly push their claims to the limit of truth – and sometimes well beyond.

15. Left to their own devices, advertisers will eagerly push their claims to the limits of truth, and often well beyond

Consequently, advertisers' freedoms could not remain wholly unconstrained. A landmark case occurred in 1891, when a Mrs Carlill bought a 'Carbolic Smoke Bomb' whose advertisement guaranteed protection against influenza (and many other illnesses), or £100 reward. The Smoke Bomb bombed. Mrs Carlill caught the 'flu, sued for her £100 under Common Law, and won.

The court viewed the advertisement as a contract. Thereafter, the UK Sale of Goods Act was passed in 1893, which greatly increased consumers' civil remedies over and above those provided by the Common Law. The 20th century saw a continuing escalation of the legal power of consumers, against advertisers.

For members of the public, however, taking errant advertisers to court is a time-consuming and costly business – and there is no guarantee the complainant will win the case. It quickly became apparent that the public needed to be protected by an advertising control system far less ponderous, and less expensive, than solicitors and courts. Even before the Second World War, pressure built up for the advertising industry to put its house in order, and to regulate itself. In 1927, the UK Advertising Association set up the first self-regulatory National Vigilance Committee, which a year later was expanded into the Advertising Investigation Department (AID). Though puny by today's standards, the AID helped drive shady operators out of business, persuaded agencies to stop handling fraudulent advertisers' campaigns, and dealt with 1,169 complaints from the public in 12 months during 1936–7.

After the Second World War, once Western economies were thriving again, from the 1960s onwards, consumerism – consumers lobbying for better trading standards and for consumer protection – grew apace. In 1962, the first Advertising Standards Authority (ASA) was set up to handle consumer complaints about advertising. But it soon became clear this ASA was a toothless tiger. It was underfunded, and therefore understaffed, and its powers were nominal. Just over a decade later, in 1974, Britain found itself with a socialist government led by left-wing Prime Minister Harold Wilson. Wilson scorned advertising, believing it to be a waste of economic resources (as did many economists at this time). In 1974, the advertising industry was warned by the government that if it did not control non-television advertising as effectively as television was already controlled, new laws would be enacted which would force it to do so. As we have seen, the print media's dislike of government controls is buried deep in their DNA, so this threat spurred the print media, and advertisers, into an immediate response.

In 1975, a far larger, and far better funded, Advertising Standards Authority opened for business. The money was raised – and is still raised – by a 0.1% levy on all advertising expenditure, paid by advertisers and collected by their agencies. Its independence from pressure by advertisers was built into its fundamental structure. In cooperation with the advertising industry, and with the approval of the government, Codes of Advertising Practice were written, and these are regularly updated. It is the ASA's role to enforce these Codes, and it was not long before the new ASA showed its claws, in a series of tough decisions against misleading and dishonest advertisers. Public and political respect for the ASA grew apace, and its powers have since been consistently extended. In the early 1990s, direct mail and direct marketing were brought under the ASA's wing. In 2004, television and radio advertising regulation was entrusted to it, a complete reversal of the situation in earlier years. And today, most Internet advertising also comes within its control. A levy of 0.1% does not sound that much – it isn't that much – but it raises around £10 million annually. Consequently, the ASA's highly trained staff of more than 100 people is able to deal with over 25,000 public complaints against advertising each year – of which fewer than 10% normally prove justified.

The ASA is now widely regarded as an exemplar of enlightened self-regulation, both in advertising and outside of advertising, in Britain and throughout the world.

Brands and bad habits

Successful though it has been, the ASA deals only with individual advertisements, on a one-by-one basis, deciding whether they infringe the Codes of Advertising Practice. This system, however, sidesteps questions relating to the advertising of entire product groups: alcohol, for example, or fast cars, or fatty foods – or cigarettes. Consideration of the role of entire advertising sectors remains the responsibility of governments.

From the early 1960s onwards, cigarettes were the advertising *cause célèbre* on which political, medical, and public attention focused. Advertising and smoking first became an issue in March 1962, when the Royal College of Physicians published its 'Smoking and Health' report. Two years later, in January 1964, the US Surgeon General published his own report on the connections between smoking and health. Both reports established a close correlation between smoking and serious illnesses, especially lung cancer, and both called for a ban on cigarette advertising to children. In Britain, this resulted in a call for a total ban on television advertising. Such a ban would be fairly easy to enact because television advertising was statutorily controlled. A ban on advertising in other media would need parliamentary legislation, which the government knew the press would fight tooth-and-nail. Parliament therefore baulked at the latter, but cigarette advertising on UK television was stopped on 1 August 1965. At that time, the Minister of Health opined in Parliament: 'I rather doubt whether this intensification of the campaign (against smoking) will result in any sudden or dramatic drop in cigarette consumption.' He was right: cigarette smoking continued to rise in Britain until the mid-1970s.

Cigarettes were not the only goods, or services, banned from advertising on television. Nor were they even, as cigarette advertising protagonists frequently claimed, the only goods banned on television which could be legally bought and sold. Breath-testing devices, matrimonial agencies, fortune tellers, undertakers, and even (at that time) charities and gambling, as well as politics and religion – all of which could be legally advertised in other media – had been banned from commercial television from its start. But it was not unreasonable to view cigarettes as a special case. Nothing similar had ever occurred in Britain before. Cigarettes were a highly popular, mass consumer product used by the majority of the population, providing income and employment to hundreds of thousands of people, perhaps millions indirectly, and heavily taxed, thus providing the state with considerable cash to help underwrite many social needs. There was no evidence that banning television advertising would do any good at all. In imposing the ban, the government was feigning social responsibility while in reality engaging in a cosmetic gesture to appease vociferous pressure groups. And as it turned out, the ban achieved little or nothing. In the years that followed, health warnings appeared on packs and advertisements, government anti-smoking campaigns were run frequently, and a constant stream of medical reports publicized the dangers of smoking. In the end, the only measures that truly made people smoke less were massive tax increases, which made smoking unaffordable, and bans on smoking in public places. Despite all of which, about 10 million people in Britain still smoke, almost 25% of the adult population, nearly half a century after the ban on television advertising.

Underlying the debates about smoking are fundamental questions about the influence of commercial advertising on social behaviour. To what extent can bans on advertising realize social engineering goals? Pressure groups everywhere in the world believe that alcohol advertising makes people drink more, car advertising makes people speed, toy advertising makes kids pester their parents, fast food and confectionery advertising makes kids (and adults) obese, slimming advertising makes girls anorexic, and medicine advertising makes people hypochondriac. It seems perverse – not to say self-serving – for the advertising industry to deny all this. If advertising does not increase these habits, and these markets, why do advertisers advertise?

16. Does alcohol advertising make people drink more?

At the close of the 20th century, as these sectoral attacks
were growing in number and frequency, the UK Advertising
Association Economics Committee responded by researching and
publishing a report titled *Does Advertising Affect Market Size?*
The objective was to determine whether, for example, advertising

for alcohol brands truly does make people drink more (or make more people drink), toy advertising truly does make parents spend more – or toilet soap advertising makes people wash more. As with many such advertising studies, there was no simple, definitive answer. To quote the report:

> There is always the possibility that advertising affects the size of a particular market, but its scale and significance are highly variable.

Brand advertising, the study showed, rarely increases the size of a market (or product sector) if the market is large, long-established, static, and satisfies a basic need. Nor do advertisers expect otherwise. Toilet soap advertisers do not expect their advertising to make people wash more, any more than petfood advertisers expect people to buy more pets or feed them more. Nor do newspapers, when they advertise themselves, hope people will read more papers. In all those cases, and countless others, the aim of the advertiser is to increase market share, at the expense of competitors. And that is precisely what the advertising – if it works at all – achieves.

On the other hand, in markets (or product categories) that are small, or new, or are already growing, brand advertising does appear to fuel growth, and gets more people to use the product, or gets people who already use the product to use it more. New electrical and electronic gadgets and equipment, for example, fall into this latter category, as do new snacks and hobby products. Once again, what happens is not accidental. In such markets, the advertiser wants to stimulate growth, because as the market becomes larger, the sales of all the brands within it increase commensurately.

But most of the products and practices that the pressure groups want to ban from advertising – alcohol, 'junk foods', advertising to children, and so on – fall straight into the former category: large, static, well-established markets. That is why the bans are ineffective. It is worth pointing out that when advertisers deliberately aim *to increase* the sales of large, static, well-established products – as they have tried to do for milk, eggs, and meat in the past, for example – those campaigns have been equally ineffective. Once society has made its mind up about a particular product, over many years and often centuries, advertising is not nearly a sufficiently powerful force to make people change their minds. Advertising can most definitely sell brands, but its role in social engineering is minimal, if it exists at all. (It is true that advertising has helped discourage drunken driving. But, as with smoking, the advertising was backed by strong legislation, police activity, breathalysers, and relentless press publicity. Advertising alone would never have done the trick.)

Chapter 9
The role of advertising in society

'Do you think advertising is a moral activity', I recently asked the 30 or so graduates I was addressing at a seminar. The graduates had been working in advertising agencies for two or three years. There was a stony silence.

'What do you mean by a moral activity?', one of them asked, eventually.

'Well ... do you think advertising really does good for the general public, for ordinary people, for men and women in the street?'

The graduates looked bewildered.

'There's the "Don't Drink and Drive" campaign', someone eventually said thoughtfully. 'That does good. That's moral.'

'And the Give Blood ads', piped up someone else. 'They're good too. And some charity adverts I suppose.'

'Anything else?', I asked hopefully. But that was it. Nobody could think of any other advertising which they thought moral, or which did any good for the general public, the men and women in the street. I felt profoundly depressed. Here was a group of lively young people, about to spend their lives working in an industry which, as far as they were concerned, provides almost no worthwhile benefits to society. With the exception of a few government and charity campaigns – a minuscule proportion of total advertising – they could think of nothing morally good to say about their chosen career.

As we have seen, they are not alone. They were all well educated, with good degrees from good universities. Most educated, intellectual people are innately hostile to aspects of advertising. Some, like Lord Reith, are innately hostile to all aspects of advertising. It would be astonishing if anyone as hostile to advertising as Reith would choose to work in the industry. But without being as hostile as Reith, many of those who work in advertising have personal qualms about their job. And whether or not they personally have qualms, they soon become used to being verbally attacked by advertising's critics at social events – and quite adept at answering such critics, and fending off their attacks, whatever their own qualms.

However, few of them are much good at turning the criticisms on their head, and showing advertising to be a highly worthwhile, indeed moral, business – a business that ordinary men and women in the street benefit from directly, every day, in countless ways. People in advertising get pretty good at defensively arguing that it does little, if any, harm, but – as the graduates at the seminar demonstrated – they seem unable to show it does any positive good. Yet it does.

As we saw in the first chapter, advertising involves a tripartite of three different groups – plus, in fact, a crucial fourth group, unmentioned in that chapter. The tripartite groups mentioned are the advertisers, who spend the money; the media, who get about 90% of the money the advertisers spend; and the agencies, who create the campaigns, buy the media – and make it all happen, for the remaining 10%.

Which, then, is the crucial fourth group involved in advertising? The fourth group is the general public, the consumers, the ordinary men and women in the street who are (or are not) influenced by the advertisements. This is the group the critics are usually concerned about when they question the morality and benefits of advertising. But this group is not wholly separate to, or different from, the other groups. All four groups overlap and interact: they are generally the same people, with different hats on – the same members of society, in different aspects of their lives. However, to analyse its morality, it is essential to explore how advertising affects people – affects all of us – when we are wearing these different hats.

Advertising helps employees

Let's begin, then, with the advertisers. In the context of morality, the advertisers concerned are usually large companies. Nobody would claim that large companies always behave perfectly. But equally, nobody would deny that there are two things large companies have to do supremely well, if they are to stay in business over the long term. They have to employ and manage sizable numbers of employees, and they have to make profits. So the majority of those men and women in the street earn their pay, or are in the families of those who earn their pay, from major advertisers. In short, they earn their money – for their food, their clothes, and everything else – from the large companies, the major advertisers.

It might be, of course, that the money the large companies spend on advertising is unnecessary, is wasted. In the past, there undeniably were economists who believed advertising is ineffective, and is therefore a waste of resources. Today such economists are few and far between. Over recent decades, countless econometric studies, from all around the world, have established beyond further argument that advertising works. Precisely how well advertising works varies from campaign to campaign, as we saw in the section on the IPA Advertising Effectiveness Awards. But overall, as the IPA Awards prove, advertising creates demand. What does this mean for ordinary men and women on the street? It means employment. Demand creates sales, sales create jobs; no sales, no jobs. Companies cannot employ people unless consumers buy the goods and services those people produce. And more sales mean more jobs. Putting it like that is a tad simplistic, but it is fundamentally true – as any business leader or economist will confirm.

Moreover, when they have jobs, they pay taxes: taxes that fund government expenditure on education, health, law and order, and all the other social amenities we value. Taxes that pay the salaries of all those who work for the government, providing those social amenities. So no consumer demand means no sales, no jobs, no taxes, no social amenities. Naturally, advertising does not do all of this on its own. But it makes a powerful and positive contribution: it helps keep the wheels of industry spinning.

And it helps companies make profits, the profits on which their long-term existence depends. Again, as we have seen, the precise profit advertising generates will vary from company to company, from campaign to campaign. And profits not only keep the companies in business, they are a major contributor to taxes – to more social amenities; and company profits fund investment, to create more jobs in the future – making the wheels spin faster and longer.

So this is the first of advertising's key contributions to society: when people are wearing their workwear hats, advertising creates jobs and all the benefits that flow from them. Maybe this explains why there is no successful economy in the world where there is no advertising.

And while talking about jobs, it is worth noting that approximately one-third of all employees find their jobs as a result of seeing and responding to advertisements. This may not be part of the main debate about the morality of advertising, but it is a substantial benefit to society.

Advertising helps media users

Let's turn to the media, which receive the 90% or so of all advertisers' expenditure. How does this help ordinary people? Well, first, in the UK it provides them with roughly two-thirds of all their broadcast media, absolutely free. In other countries, like the USA, this figure reaches 100% of all broadcast media. And advertising heavily subsidizes the Internet, so that most websites are available either without cost or at a fraction of their set-up and running costs. The digital media revolution, upon which we are all so dependent, has been provided to us for very nearly nothing – paid for by advertising. This is a totally new public benefit.

But advertising's benefits to the media, and thus to society, go wider and much deeper. More than 3,000 consumer magazines are published in Britain. Each one is of personal interest to groups of readers, large or small. And each one is heavily subsidized by advertising, so that its readers – all those men and all those women in all those streets – buy it at a small percentage of its production cost. And research shows that many readers of special interest magazines find the advertisements at least as helpful and interesting as the editorial itself. Some magazines contain only advertisements, with no editorial whatsoever: living proof that their readers value the advertising they contain. As with magazines, so it is with almost all other advertising media, from cinemas to public transport: the revenue they receive from advertising reduces, even if only marginally, the prices they charge the public for what they provide.

But we have not yet got to the most significant media benefit of all. Advertising provides societies with an open, influential, and politically independent press. Without advertising, the price of newspapers would rocket. Then their circulations would plummet. Then the prices would rocket again. The outcome? Our diverse and competitive local and national press would shrivel. Newspapers are already under heavy competition from the Internet. Without any advertising subsidy, many newspapers would close down. A ridiculous thought? Not at all.

Politicians, in all countries, often seek to control the media – successfully and brutally in non-democratic autocracies. In democracies, their efforts to control the media have to be more subtle. As was noted on page 19, in order to control the press, in 1712 British politicians imposed a duty of one shilling on every advertisement published in newspapers. The politicians' aim was deliberately to cut the newspapers' advertising revenue, in order to make the papers more expensive and thus stop people – particularly poorer people – from reading them. This was one of several taxes designed to restrain the power of the press. The advertising tax was steadily increased, and was not abandoned until 1853. As intended, it helped hold back the development of a free press in Britain for almost 150 years. A politically free and critical press, unfettered by any dependence on government finance, is one of the strongest protectors of individual liberty. Advertising plays a vital role in this.

As with advertisers, nobody would claim the media are perfect. But without advertising, the media would be far weaker, far smaller, and almost certainly far more expensive. And the public, now wearing their media-receiving hats, would be far worse off.

Advertising helps national creativity

You will rightly think this is the least contentious area of the debate. Advertising inevitably helps advertising agencies – the smallest sector of the tripartite – as they would not exist without advertising. And advertising agencies are, inherently, founts of creativity.

But this contributes indirect benefits to society too. The agencies provide many serious artists and writers with a regular salary, so they can paint and write their own works. Numerous writers and artists worked in agencies before becoming established in their own right. Many great painters were also great poster artists. Exactly the same is true of film directors, many of whom learned their cinematographic craft making commercials. The agencies provide creative employment not only for the writers and art directors who work directly for them, but also provide employment to a vast hinterland of freelance creative people: photographers, designers, film directors, lighting and cameramen, actors, set designers, lettering artists – as well as those who produce the hardware for all their output: printers, film manufacturers and processors, display and set builders. Together, this sprawling creative network feeds ideas and originality into the nation's creativity, catalysing a cauldron of innovation in both the commercial and the pure arts, from which society benefits immensely.

Moreover, the public – wearing its imaginary 'aesthetic hat' – benefits directly from the agencies' work, as many advertisements succeed in being amusing, clever, witty, charming, striking, and sometimes even beautiful. This was well expressed as long ago as 1896, in a Hamburg Poster Exhibition Catalogue:

> Art should be accessible to everyone...not only to those who can afford to buy works of art or have the time to seek them out in galleries...Art must go on the streets, where chance will bring it to the notice of many thousands on their way to work who have neither the time nor money to spare. High ethical standards are fulfilled by posters created for everyday practical purposes – provided they are good posters.

A perfect description of yet another way in which advertising benefits the men and women in the street. But now we must come to the kernel of the moral question.

Advertising helps the public

This is the trickiest part. Showing how employees and their families (that's nearly everyone), and media-users (that's nearly everyone), and national creativity (that involves nearly everyone) all benefit from advertising is relatively straightforward. But does advertising really help when people are wearing their fourth hat, as consumers? Or does it, as the critics have long contended, merely manipulate them? Part of the problem here is that when it comes to consumers, to talk about 'advertising' is misleading. Consumers do not respond to advertising. They respond to advertisements. And, as has been emphasized throughout this book, advertisements are extremely diverse. So the benefits consumers derive from them are equally diverse.

Let us begin with information: we live, it is often said, in an information society. And economists have long justified advertising as a source of information. Certainly the public obtains a great deal of important and helpful information from advertisements.

Take prices. Nowadays, as we have seen, many of the largest advertisers are retailers, and the great majority of retail advertisements promote low prices. Not only is this information directly helpful for shoppers, it indirectly drives prices down. When one supermarket promotes its low prices for certain goods, other supermarkets swiftly retaliate by cutting their own prices – otherwise they know they will lose customers. Overall, prices fall. For the public, this is a pretty good deal.

At the same time, the quality of many of the goods and services we buy is constantly being improved, however slightly. Consumers benefit by getting information about these improvements from advertisements. And, once again, this forces competitors to retaliate by making quality improvements of their own. It is a continuous process. As with price-based advertising, this stimulates competition, and the public reaps the rewards.

Then there are completely new products. The public gets its information about new products in a multitude of ways, but none is faster or simpler than advertising. And there are endless occasions when consumers are searching for something – a new car, or a kid's birthday present, or an ointment to treat their spots – and advertisements tell them what is on offer. For consumers, this is all helpful information.

But it still begs one big question. How does the public benefit from advertisements that contain little or no information – particularly if these advertisements are for things the public knows about already? Information-lite advertisements include a great swathe of brand advertising, from Heineken to Heinz, from Kellogg's to Kit Kat, from Persil to Perrier. So how do consumers benefit from advertisements that provide them with almost no information at all?

In a couple of ways, at least. First, memories fail – or anyway need jogging. Everyone needs to be reminded about brands they like, but which slip from their minds. Awareness and tracking studies constantly show how quickly people forget about a brand once its advertising stops. Second, marketplaces are not static. Consumers' needs change all the time as they progress through life's stages, and though they may learn of the existence of a brand when young, they may not need to use it until they are older. An information-lite memory-jogging advertisement is often sufficient to do the trick.

Finally, getting back to the graduates at the seminar, there are specific areas of advertising which incontestably help society. Most government campaigns, charity campaigns, and pressure group campaigns bring worthwhile causes to the public's attention. All these areas of advertising have grown in recent years. They are not the basic moral justification for advertising – but they unquestionably make their contribution.

A burgeoning world of choice

Advertising today must be seen in the context of a world of immense variety and choice. In economies where there is no choice, there is no need for advertising. But in modern, affluent societies, the average large supermarket offers shoppers about 40,000 different lines; there are some 2,000 new models of car available; plus an uncountable number of consumer durables, fashions, electronic widgets, entertainments, holidays, financial investments – the list goes on and on. People need to be able to sort out all these choices reasonably swiftly and simply. Advertisements help them select the things they want, and reject those they don't, without spending forever on the task – and without going crazy.

None of this will refute the arguments of those who are against particular advertising sectors. People who want to ban advertising of tobacco, or alcohol, or advertising to children will not be persuaded their views are wrong simply because advertising is generally beneficial. But equally, their specific concerns, whether or not you agree with them, do not affect the broader case for advertising.

So what is the role of advertising in society? It creates employment, now and in the future; it provides the public with numerous free and inexpensive media; it supports media independence; it supplies shoppers with a great deal of helpful information; it pushes prices down and quality up; it keeps the public aware of all the different brands available; it helps them select from the vast range of choices modern economies offer – and it does most of this creatively, and cost-effectively. Perhaps all this should suffice to make the graduates feel that if they do spend their lives working in advertising, well, their lives will indeed have been worthwhile.

Further reading

Important classics

Claude Hopkins, *Scientific Advertising* (MacGibbon and Kee, 1968; first published 1923).
Martin Mayer, *Madison Avenue USA* (Penguin, 1960).
David Ogilvy, *Confessions of an Advertising Man* (Atheneum, 1963).
Vance Packard, *The Hidden Persuaders* (Penguin, 1960).
Rosser Reeves, *Reality in Advertising* (Alfred Knopf, 1961).

General history

John Barnicoat, *Posters: A Concise History* (Thames and Hudson, 1997).
Leonard de Vries and James Laver, *Victorian Advertisements* (John Murray, 1968).
Leonard de Vries and Ilonka Van Amstel, *American Advertisements 1865–1900* (John Murray, 1973).
Winston Fletcher, *Powers of Persuasion: The Inside Story of British Advertising 1951–2000* (Oxford University Press, 2008).
Stephen Fox, *The Mirror Makers: A History of American Advertising and its Creators* (University of Illinois Press, 1997).
Brian Henry (ed.), *British Television Advertising: The First 30 Years* (Century Benham, 1986).
Terry R. Nevett, *Advertising in Britain: A History* (William Heinemann, 1982).
Mark Tungate, *Adland: A Global History of Advertising* (Kogan Page, 2007).
E. S. Turner, *The Shocking History of Advertising* (Michael Joseph, 1951).

Marketing and branding

Tim Ambler, *Marketing and the Bottom Line* (Financial Times/ Prentice Hall, 2003).

A. S. C. Ehrenberg, *Repeat Buying* (Charles Griffin, 1988).

Stephen King, *A Master Class in Brand Planning*, ed. Judie Lannon and Merry Baskin (John Wiley, 2007).

Naomi Klein, *No Logo* (HarperCollins, 2000).

Theodore Levitt, *The Marketing Imagination* (Macmillan, 1983).

Marketing Pocket Books (Advertising Association with World Advertising Research Center, annually).

Wally Olins, *Corporate Identity* (Thames and Hudson, 1989).

Agencies and creativity

Jeremy Bullmore, *Behind the Scenes in Advertising* (World Advertising Research Center, 2003).

Design and Art Directors' Awards Annuals, 1964– .

Ivan Fallon, *The Brothers* (Hutchinson, 1988).

Winston Fletcher, *Tantrums and Talent* (Admap Publications, 1999).

Jeremy Myerson and Graham Vickers, *Rewind: Forty Years of Design and Advertising* (Phaidon, 2002).

John Ritchie and John Salmon, *Inside Collett, Dickenson and Pearce* (Batsford, 2000).

Media and Internet

Harry Henry, *The Dynamics of the British Press 1961–1984* (Advertising Association, 1986).

John W. Hobson, *The Selection of Advertising Media* (IPA, 1955).

Interactive Advertising Bureau, http://www.iab.net

Nigel T. Packer, *Internet Marketing: Strategies for Online Success* (New Holland Publishers, 2009).

Godfrey Parkin, *Digital Marketing* (Elliot Right Way Books, 2008).

Advertising effectiveness

Simon Broadbent, *Accountable Advertising* (NTC Publications, 1997).

Charles Channon (ed.), *20 Advertising Case Histories* (Cassell, 1989).

Russell H. Colley, *Defining Advertising Goals for Measured Advertising Results* (Association of American National Advertisers, first published 1961).

Winston Fletcher, *A Glittering Haze* (NTC Publications, 1992).

Giep Franzen, *Advertising Effectiveness: Findings from Empirical Research* (NTC Publications, 1994).

Laurence Green (ed.), *Advertising Works and How* (IPA and World Advertising Research Center, 2005).

World Advertising Research Center, http://www.warc.com, 1999–.

Index

Advertising

Visit the
VERY SHORT
INTRODUCTIONS
Web site

www.oup.co.uk/vsi

➤ **Information** about all published titles

➤ News of **forthcoming books**

➤ **Extracts** from the books, including titles not yet published

➤ **Reviews** and views

➤ **Links** to other **web sites** and main OUP web page

➤ Information about **VSIs in translation**

➤ **Contact** the editors

➤ **Order** other **VSIs** on-line

CLASSICS
A Very Short Introduction
Mary Beard and John Henderson

This Very Short Introduction to Classics links a haunting temple on a lonely mountainside to the glory of ancient Greece and the grandeur of Rome, and to Classics within modern culture – from Jefferson and Byron to Asterix and Ben-Hur.

'The authors show us that Classics is a "modern" and sexy subject. They succeed brilliantly in this regard ... nobody could fail to be informed and entertained – and the accent of the book is provocative and stimulating.'

John Godwin, *Times Literary Supplement*

'Statues and slavery, temples and tragedies, museum, marbles, and mythology – this provocative guide to the Classics demystifies its varied subject-matter while seducing the reader with the obvious enthusiasm and pleasure which mark its writing.'

Edith Hall

MUSIC
A Very Short Introduction
Nicholas Cook

This stimulating Very Short Introduction to music
invites us to really *think* about music and the values
and qualities we ascribe to it.

'A *tour de force*. Nicholas Cook is without doubt one of
the most probing and creative thinkers about music we
have today.'
Jim Samson, University of Bristol

'Nicholas Cook offers a perspective that is clearly influenced by recent writing in a host of disciplines related
to music. It may well prove a landmark in the appreciation of the topic ... In short, I can hardly imagine it being
done better.'
Roger Parker, University of Cambridge

www.oup.co.uk/vsi/music

BUDDHISM
A Very Short Introduction
Damien Keown

From its origin in India over two thousand years
ago Buddhism has spread throughout Asia and is now
exerting an increasing influence on western culture. In
clear and straightforward language, and with the help of
maps, diagrams and illustrations, this book explains how
Buddhism began and how it evolved into its present-day
form. The central teachings and practices are set out
clearly, and keys topics such as karma and rebirth, medi-
tation, ethics, and Buddhism in the West receive detailed
coverage in separate chapters. The distinguishing fea-
tures of the main schools – such as Tibetan and Zen
Buddhism – are clearly explained. The book will be
of interest to anyone seeking a sound basic
understanding of Buddhism.

> 'Damien Keown's book is a readable and wonderfully
> lucid introduction to one of mankind's most beautiful,
> profound, and compelling systems of wisdom. His
> impressive powers of explanation help us to come to
> terms with a vital contemporary reality.'
>
> **Bryan Appleyard**

www.oup.co.uk/vsi/buddhism

LITERARY THEORY
A Very Short Introduction
Jonathan Culler

Literary Theory is a controversial subject. Said to have transformed the study of culture and society in the past two decades, it is accused of undermining respect for tradition and truth, encouraging suspicion about the political and psychological implications of cultural products instead of admiration for great literature. In this Very Short Introduction, Jonathan Culler explains 'theory', not by describing warring 'schools' but by sketching key 'moves' that theory has encouraged and speaking directly about the implications of cultural theory for thinking about literature, about the power of language, and about human identity. This lucid introduction will be useful for anyone who has wondered what all the fuss is about or who wants to think about literature today.

> 'It is impossible to imagine a clearer treatment of the subject, or one that is, within the given limits of length, more comprehensive. Culler has always been remarkable for his expository skills, and here he has found exactly the right method and tone for his purposes.'
>
> **Frank Kermode**

www.oup.co.uk/vsi/literarytheory

HINDUISM
A Very Short Introduction
Kim Knott

Hinduism is practised by eighty per cent of India's
population, and by thirty million people outside India.
In this Very Short Introduction, Kim Knott combines a
succinct and authoritative overview of a major religion
with an analysis of the challenges facing it in the twentieth
century. She discusses key preoccupations of Hinduism
such as the centrality of the *Veda* as religious texts, the
role of brahmins, gurus, and storytellers in the transmission of divine truths, and the importance of epics such as
the *Ramayana*. Issues such as the place of women and
dalits (untouchables) in contemporary society are also
addressed, making this book stimulating reading for
Hindus and non-Hindus alike.

www.oup.co.uk/vsi/hinduism